Prayer Pattern

Spiritual Truths for Breakthrough
ONCE AND FOR ALL!

TRACY L. WARD

WESTBOW
P R E S S®
A DIVISION OF THOMAS NELSON
& ZONDERVAN

This book is a work of non-fiction. Unless otherwise noted, the author and the publisher make no explicit guarantees as to the accuracy of the information contained in this book and in some cases, names of people and places have been altered to protect their privacy.

Scripture quotations taken from the New American Standard Bible®, Copyright © 1960, 1962, 1963, 1968, 1971, 1972, 1973, 1975, 1977, 1995 by The Lockman Foundation. Used by permission. (www.Lockman.org)

Scripture taken from the New King James Version. Copyright © 1979, 1980, 1982 by Thomas Nelson, Inc. Used by permission. All rights reserved.

WestBow Press books may be ordered through booksellers or by contacting:

WestBow Press
A Division of Thomas Nelson & Zondervan
1663 Liberty Drive
Bloomington, IN 47403
www.westbowpress.com
1 (866) 928-1240

Because of the dynamic nature of the Internet, any web addresses or links contained in this book may have changed since publication and may no longer be valid. The views expressed in this work are solely those of the author and do not necessarily reflect the views of the publisher, and the publisher hereby disclaims any responsibility for them.

Any people depicted in stock imagery provided by Shutterstock are models, and such images are being used for illustrative purposes only. Certain stock imagery © Shutterstock.

ISBN: 978-1-5127-3724-0 (sc)
ISBN: 978-1-5127-3725-7 (hc)
ISBN: 978-1-5127-3723-3 (e)

Library of Congress Control Number: 2016937791

Print information available on the last page.

WestBow Press rev. date: 04/27/2016

Dedication and Thanks

Prayer Pattern is dedicated to Father God, Christ Jesus, and the amazing Holy Spirit. The Holy Trinity inspired and pushed me to write this book to help believers and nonbelievers come into the knowledge of their inheritance in Christ Jesus, and thus, enter into the fullness of the plans and purposes that God has for them. I thank my wonderful husband for his incredible support, generosity and encouragement during this writing project. I thank my sister for allowing God to rescue her and bring her back into the family fold and for her willingness to submit to Holy Spirit as He transforms her into everything that God has written in His book for her. My sister's transparency and willingness to share her transformation will help millions gain the hope that they, too, can step into everything God has planned for them- no matter how bad the situation may look on the surface.

I thank my mom, my mate, who has faithfully been on the prayer call daily for the last two years, and who helped me bring this book to fruition. I am beyond thankful that we have drawn ever closer through this amazing process. I could not have done this without her. Lastly, I want to thank my dad for taking a leap of faith to join me, my mom, my 92-year-old grandmother, my niece, my two sisters, and other friends and family who regularly join our daily prayer calls. Although my dad initially stepped way outside of his comfort zone, our family has watched him blossom and grow in the confidence of the Lord as he boldly declares over our family, our church, our city, and the nations.

1 Chronicles 28:19

"All this," said David, "the Lord made me understand in writing by His hand upon me, all the details of this pattern."

Contents

Preface

W hat I am about to say may sound like a grandiose statement, but I believe without a shadow of a doubt that this book was inspired by God Himself. Let me explain. In early 2014, my mom and dad received a devastating phone call from a family member, to whom I'll refer to as Robert, regarding my sister's behavior and how she had slipped into an even worse condition than what had been reported three months prior, which was bad then. Robert indicated that he was afraid for her life and was starting to believe that if things kept going in the direction they were headed, he may one day receive a call that she was found in a Dumpster.

When my mom shared this with my youngest sister, she recalled a childhood fear that this same sister might die an early death; consequently, she shared the same sentiment as Robert. At this point, great fear began to creep in on the scene. Over the last thirty years, this sister has unfortunately dealt with numerous behavioral issues, but this specific bout seemed to bring about a particularly high level of concern.

When my mom called to tell me about all of this, I could sense the distress in her voice. She asked what I thought, and for an instant, I felt the twinges of fear begin to rise in me, but Holy Spirit helped nip that in the bud. I had a quick revelation that Robert and my younger sister were looking through *lenses of fear* and, therefore, the only thing they could see was my sister in a Dumpster. He also showed me that both fear and faith are extremely contagious and that my mom and I needed to carefully guard our hearts, reject fear, stand in faith, and most important, *trust God*! After all, the Bible is very clear when it comes to trusting God: Jeremiah 17:7–8 says, *"Blessed is the man who trusts in the Lord*, and whose hope is the Lord. For he shall be like a tree planted by the waters, which spreads out its roots by the river, *and will not fear when heat comes*; but its leaf will be green, *and will not be anxious in the year of drought, nor will cease from yielding fruit*" (emphasis added). It was clear—we had to trust God on this one.

From there, God gave my mom and me some very specific strategies on how we were to navigate the mess that was before us, because in the natural, we had no idea how to approach this situation. The good news was that God knew exactly what was going to happen and that the victory was ours before we even got started. The amazing part is that with the Prayer Pattern that He would later give us, not only would it permanently change our family's lives once and for all, but it would also serve as a blueprint for other believers around the world struggling to overcome their own uncertain or hopeless situations.

Introduction

And you shall know the truth, and the truth shall make you free. (John 8:32)

To the Christian

P *rayer Pattern* was especially written for today's Christians. Since 2005, my heart and passion has been to see every believer come to know his or her glorious inheritance through Christ Jesus and to walk in the victory that He so richly afforded us when He sat down at the right hand of the Father. Unfortunately, I have witnessed too many Christians become completely overwhelmed by their circumstances and subsequently wind up becoming prime targets of the enemy. Regarding the situation with my sister, my mom and I came to realize that we willingly allowed the Enemy to use our backs for target practice; but by the grace of God, we decided that enough was enough and too much stinks!

We give all the glory to God for showing us what to do about my sister's terrible situation and how to fix it, and that is why *Prayer Pattern* was written. I believe that every person who identifies him- or herself as a Christ follower needs to read this book, especially if you have asked yourself any of the following questions or can identify with any of the following statements:

- I'm not sure how to handle this situation.
- I thought God would have answered my prayer by now. How much longer?

- I'm not sure if this will ever change.
- Why isn't God answering my prayers?
- Is this the best God has for me?
- I'm not sure I even know how to pray.
- I hate seeing the people I love in bondage, and it seems my prayers are not working.
- There's got to be more to this "prayer thing."
- God hasn't answered my prayers regarding one or more situations, and I'm starting to have doubts about all of this.
- I see God moving in others' lives but not mine.
- I need to experience breakthrough. *Help*!
- I am angry with God because He hasn't answered my prayers.
- I can't do this anymore.
- I've completely given up hope.
- I'm now questioning whether I'm a Christian or not.
- Because God has not answered my prayers, I'm leaving the faith.

I fully recognize that some of these questions or statements may seem extreme, but countless numbers of Christians have left the faith because their prayers went completely unanswered and they therefore felt let down by God. By the grace of God, I believe Prayer Pattern will address many of the issues that Christians face with regard to unanswered prayer, and furthermore, it will teach you about your identity in Christ, your inheritance, the Helper, the mighty weapons in your arsenal, the truth about the devil, and the most powerful prayer strategy that you may ever encounter. Be encouraged and know that God has wonderful things in store for His sons and daughters, and my desire is for you to come into the *full knowledge* of all that He has for you!

... that the God of our Lord Jesus Christ, the Father of glory, may give to you the spirit of wisdom and revelation in the knowledge of Him, the eyes of your understanding being enlightened; that you may know what is the hope of His calling, what are the riches of the glory of His inheritance in the saints, and what is the exceeding greatness of His power toward us who believe, according to the working of His mighty power. (Eph. 1:17–19)

To the Non-Christian

What if you say that you are not a Christ follower? Well, you should probably read *Prayer Pattern* anyway, but let me tell you why. Although you may not be a Christian, there are still issues in your life that may be beyond your ability to adequately respond to or manage. What do you do when that happens? Let's face it—all people encounter situations that will bring great stress, anxiety, and feelings of helplessness. If you think about it, those are the kinds of situations that lead people to abuse drugs, alcohol, and prescription medications; participate in reckless activities; commit crimes; abandon families; and if things really get bad, take their own lives. Why go through that when God offered His Son as a living sacrifice so that we can live an overcoming life here on earth and everlasting life afterward? Besides, God loves you like crazy!

The Christian Difference

The difference in the Christian faith is that when you accept Christ as your personal Lord and Savior, you have access to *all* of God's kingdom resources, and those abundant resources are more than sufficient to help you manage every single circumstance you will ever face. One of the greatest resources that God gave believers was the ability to pray with authentic power and authority. When we have a personal relationship with Christ and we pray His will mixed with faith, then God hears our prayers and we can expect to have those prayers answered (even if the answer is no or not yet because He has something *far better* for us or He is preventing us from harm or danger that we cannot see). This is not something that I'm just pulling out of a hat; what I am saying is actually backed up by God's Word.

> These things I have written to you who believe in the name of the Son of God, so that you may know that you have eternal life. This is the confidence which we have before Him, that, if we ask anything according to His will, He hears us. And if we know that He hears us in

whatever we ask, we know that we have the requests which we have asked from Him. (1 John 5:13-15)

My last question is that *if* there might be even an ounce of truth to anything that you just read, wouldn't you at least want to know more? If so, I highly recommend reading *Prayer Pattern*!

To the Atheist

If your mind is so firmly closed when it comes to believing that there is a God, then you may not be able to stomach this book. If you refuse to give God a chance to show how much He loves you or you are unwilling to even *try* to believe that He could help you in your personal situations, then *Prayer Pattern* might bore you to tears. While this may sound a tad rude, this, too, is backed up by Scripture.

> But without faith it is impossible to please Him, for he who comes to God must believe that He is, and that He is a rewarder of those who diligently seek Him. (Heb. 11:6)

Wait—There's Hope!

Think about it, the fact that you are holding this book in your hands is evidence that God is up to *something*. Even if you fall into the non-Christian or atheist category but for some strange reason are intrigued and feel like you might be able to muster up the tiniest mustard seed of faith, then you should definitely read this book! It's pretty surprising how little faith you actually need in order for God to move. Yes, that is in the Scriptures as well.

> So the Lord said, "If you have faith as a mustard seed, you can say to this mulberry tree, 'Be pulled up by the roots and be planted in the sea,' and it would obey you." (Luke 17:6)

Last Thoughts

Let me take a moment to encourage you to invest the time to read this book, ask God to help you with those parts you don't understand with your natural mind and invite Holy Spirit to help apply Prayer Pattern to your individual situations. I am more than confident that God will move mightily on your behalf! When my mom and I first embarked on this journey regarding my sister's awful situation, we had absolutely no idea where things would go. However, in the days and weeks after we began applying the Prayer Pattern God gave us, we witnessed Him do several miraculous things; and over the next two years, we saw radical and life-changing transformation in my sister and our relationship with her, her family, and our family as a whole. Only God could have brought us to this place, and I am fully convinced that *He desires to do the same for you!*

The Power of God's Word

When my mom received that dreadful call from Robert about my sister, great concern swept through our family. Although we had no idea of how things would turn out, God surely knew! In fact, shortly after that call, God, through His Holy Spirit, spoke a word to my mom to let her know that He had things well under His control.

That same day, God told my mom to get her journal because He had a word for her in regards to the situation at hand. For over thirty years, my mom regularly receives personal words from the Lord, which she records in her journals. On that day, The Lord said:

"You are under the shelter of the Most High and you abide in the secret place. I Myself will go after your daughter and bring her back from the kingdom of darkness. I will fight this battle, and every battle I fight, I win. See her now as I see her, whole and complete, missing nothing. I am so pleased at the confidence you have in Me, the trust that you have that I will do everything that I said I will do. Not one word that I have spoken will drop to the ground. This will not be a long drawn out battle. I have accelerated this time table. Rest in Me and My ability to redeem your daughter out of the pit that she is in. Believe Me when I say that everything will be okay. Isaiah 57:18 I have seen her (willful) ways, but I will heal her; I will lead her and restore comfort to her and to those who mourn for her."

Confirmation!

What an encouraging word the Lord gave my mom, however, that word would not be seen or brought back to remembrance any time soon. In fact, it was more than six months before she would stumble across that word while looking for something else. When Mom read it, she knew that she had written it because it was her own handwriting, but she had no memory of writing it. It was dated, which was the only way she knew when it was written. Mom immediately called me and read the prophetic word given to her twelve days prior to the initiation of our prayer call. What God spoke to her six months earlier had *already* come to pass! She recalled the scripture from Jeremiah 33:3 "Call to Me and I will answer you, and I will tell you great and mighty things, which you do not know."

By that point in time, my sister had already been on our daily prayer call for the previous two months and we had seen profound changes in her and in our relationship as a family. We were overjoyed at the fulfillment of God's promise to bring her out of the kingdom of darkness, and that this was not a long drawn out battle. Transformation and deliverance began taking place with a speed that surprised us all. That powerful word gave us an even greater confidence in what God was doing in and through us on this incredible journey. We knew that this was something special and that it could only have been orchestrated by God.

The Power of the Testimony

Testimonies usually go at the end of a book, however, this is no ordinary book! This story is so powerful that it deserved to be released in the beginning rather than the end. What makes this outcome different is that God initiated the strategy, we partnered with Him through our positions of being seated with Christ in the heavenly places and declaring from that position, and then we watched Him bring about the victory.

I had always felt like an outsider in my family. From a very young age we were taught to be independent, and if we wanted something other than the basic necessities, it was up to us to get the things that we wanted. While that developed an exceptionally strong work ethic, I thought that if I had to rely on my own skills and abilities to achieve the things I desired, I didn't have to answer to anyone.

With that continued attitude, rebellion had the perfect ground to sprout and grow in my life over the years. This turned into a mindset which eventually became part of my character. At first, this led to a breakdown in my role as a daughter under the authority of my parents. Later, these breakdowns developed in other areas of my life. Needless to say, my teenage years were not fun for me or my family. I could not wait to get out on my own so that I could do exactly what I wanted to do and when I wanted to do it!

I accepted Jesus into my heart at an early age, learned to pray, and experienced miracles first hand in my life. As I became an adult, I drifted away from walking with the Lord and decided that *I* wanted to be in control of my life. I was later diagnosed with Bipolar I Disorder, which caused me to experience more of the manic manifestations of the illness than the depressive ones. This included an abundance of energy, impulsivity, and taking risks that later proved to be dangerous. These behaviors took a serious toll on my own family over the years with my husband and three children paying the price. While I was a provider financially for them, I was frequently absent emotionally. My moods were unpredictable and I was often short-tempered and impatient with them. Some of my behavior was dangerous to myself, because in the midst of a manic episode, I did not require the normal amount of sleep, and therefore, I engaged in all sorts of questionable and destructive activities. Working late at night was the norm, and unfortunately, my brain and mindset failed to take into consideration the consequences of the risk factors associated with these activities.

Owning my own businesses occupied the majority of my time and allowed me to escape the emptiness and dissatisfaction that I felt in my personal life. I didn't have time to spend with my husband and children, attend family events or go to church. I loved the work I performed and dedicated my efforts and energy in that direction. Businesswise, I experienced success, but familywise I was completely bankrupt. I didn't know what to do to change the situation because in periods of normal behavior I could see the damage I inflicted, but felt helpless to do anything about the situation.

At the time, I was unaware of the concern my husband had for my safety and well-being. We were often not on speaking terms because of my lifestyle and the breakdown of communication in our marriage. Little did I know that my mother and sister had begun praying and declaring over me. One day my husband encouraged me to attend service at my family's church and we decided to show up with our children. I didn't realize it at the time, but this was only days after my mom and sister began praying. I felt so much love there and a reconnection to something else that had been missing from my life all these years. I did not realize how much I missed walking with the Lord and hearing the voice of His Holy Spirit.

In addition, I began to see changes in my family of origin and I felt something that I never really felt before from them, true love and acceptance. I didn't really understand what it was at first, but as time went on, I was drawn to them in a way I never was before. Their devotion to pray for me daily was a sign of how much they loved me. I later learned that they had been praying and declaring over me for deliverance from Bipolar Disorder and for God to heal me from the inside out. This included emotional healing as well as normalization of any chemical imbalances. They also declared that I would no longer have to take any psychiatric medications so that I could be free from the side effects.

A few months later, I joined my mom and my sister on their daily prayer call. When I joined the call, my dad and my husband joined as well. This was so powerful! On this prayer call, I learned something radical. I learned that I was seated with Christ in the heavenly places (Ephesians 2:4-6), and because of this truth, I now had the authority and power to co-labor with God and Christ, and declare God's will *from* the heavens to earth. We listen to what Holy Spirit is saying and then we speak and release those words into the earth. We have the assurance that the words spoken will not return void, but accomplish what they are sent to do, even if those answers come later or the outcome shapes up differently than what we prayed.

Time after time, we witness miracles that occur as a result of our daily prayer calls. My youngest daughter often joins our calls and my heart is so delighted. We are both stepping into His purpose for which He created us and are doing his will on earth as it is in heaven. Our family has become so much closer and stronger. As a result of learning to operate in my inheritance, I have been speaking prophetically and walking in my calling as an evangelist. Before these events, I would have never felt comfortable praying with complete strangers and declaring over them what Holy Spirit was leading me to say. I am now able to touch people's lives for God's kingdom on a regular basis, and I could not be happier doing it!

In October of 2014, I received one of the desires of my heart. I became pregnant with my fourth child. As a result of this, I was taken off all of my medications and became free from their side effects. Although I was 44 at the time and was considered as a high risk for complications, I knew that God had something special planned for me. Holy Spirit later reminded me that my parents and my sister had boldly declared that I would be taken off all medications, and this presented the perfect opportunity for the Lord to show Himself strong. God healed me and blessed me with a healthy beautiful baby boy.

Today, a year and a half after implementing Prayer Pattern in my life, God is bringing me through the process of transformation. I am no longer the person I used to be, and each day, I step deeper into the fullness that God has planned for me. My prayer for you, the reader, is that as you embark on this journey, you will be able to use this pattern of prayer to grow closer to the Lord, learn how to pray with power and authority, and use this as a spring board to transform the situations in your life, as well as those in your sphere of influence!

Chapter 1

The Process of Resignation

So we see that they could not enter in because of unbelief. (Prov. 13:12)

Hope deferred makes the heart sick, but when the desire comes, it is a tree of life. (Heb. 3:19)

A Little History

After my mom and I processed the situation with my sister, I started wondering what had happened to us. What had happened to the days of my youth, back in the eighties, when Mom taught us to fight for a family breakthrough, those days when we were neophyte Christians and the Holy Spirit gave my mom the strategies to experience breakthrough? She subsequently taught us those strategies—living in the Word, warring in the spirit, fasting regularly, praying on our knees, and so forth. Before we invited Jesus into our lives, we had a tremendously dysfunctional family. In fact, I think we put the "D" in dysfunctional! However, with the faith we developed in our early Christian years, we boldly contended for our family, and the Lord provided the breakthrough that we so desperately needed.

What had happened to those days when we fully expected the Lord to move on our family's behalf and would pray until we saw it come to pass? We had been able to do just that in so many other areas of our lives but not for my sister. Why was that?

Maybe we had gotten beat down in the process. Maybe we had become callous and hardened over my sister's behavior. Maybe we didn't truly believe that the situation would ever change. Maybe we had gotten tired and did not know what else to do. Whatever the reason, nothing was changing. But then again, why should it have? After all, our prayers were not being said in faith, and they frequently consisted of begging and pleading, which we know does not move mountains. In the end, did we envelop ourselves in the Holy Spirit to pray for the promises God had made my mom so many years ago? No, we did not. So was all this supposed to simply change by osmosis?

Sure, I guess God could have waved His mighty hand and miraculously changed everything—He is God, and He could do that. But didn't God create us to walk in faith, believe, and declare that things change? Didn't God give us power and authority over our circumstances, give us Christ as our hope and glory, give us His Holy Spirit to guide us, and give us the assured victory to bring light and life into those dark places? Yes, He did, and my mom and I believe in and stand on those things in so many other areas of our lives. Why had we not accessed what was so freely available to us when it came to my sister? I had no answers for that question.

After realizing that we had not been walking in God's promises relative to this situation, I began thinking about the steps that had led us to this point. Mom and I came to the sad realization that over the previous thirty years, we had become ridiculously passive and apathetic and had completely lost hope for my sister's situation. Over that time, we watched her slip further and further into spiritual bondage, and we bought the lie that because her situation had always been this way, it would probably always be this way. *The Devil is a liar!*

The Process

At this point, God showed us that unbelief was the chief reason we had either stopped praying or were mindlessly praying for my sister. Proverbs 13:12 says, "So we see that they could not enter in because of unbelief." Unbelief is like the most deadly form of cancer believers could ever have. Unbelief spreads quickly, and if it is not caught and rooted out, it will begin to negatively impact other areas of a believer's life. Unbelief will keep believers from fully entering into the promises God has for us here on earth.

When we accept Jesus as our Lord and Savior, we of course receive the promise of eternal life—the assurance that we are going to heaven—but we also gain the great promise of receiving the keys of the kingdom of heaven while we are here on earth and all that goes along with those promises. "And I will give you the keys of the kingdom of heaven, and whatever you bind on earth will be bound in heaven, and whatever you loose on earth will be loosed in heaven" (Matt. 16:19). Unfortunately, unbelief keeps us from inheriting the fullness of God's kingdom, His promises, and the life of victory He intended for us.

God further revealed that in this process of resignation there were several other dangerous seeds that accompanied the seed of unbelief. He showed my mom and me that this entire process starts with an expectation or belief that He will move on our behalf in a particular circumstance. When that expectation or belief is not met, *discouragement* will start to settle in. Once discouragement takes hold, the door to *passivity* is flung wide open. Where we used to vigorously pray and believe that God was going to change the circumstance, we are now spiritually lazy, we pray less frequently, and we lack the fervor that once accompanied our prayers.

Then, *disillusionment* enters the scene, and feelings of doubt and worry become much more prominent. Once we start to become disillusioned, questions of whether God will show up or if things will ever change begin to enter our minds. Conditions are now ripe for the deadly seed of *unbelief* to take hold, and once that happens, things tend to go downhill drastically from there.

If not brought under control at this point, unbelief will develop and give birth to *apathy.* In this ungodly place, comments like "Why bother praying anymore?" "I'm not sure God even hears me," "Maybe it is meant to be this way," and other insidious little lies that go along with apathy. Once apathy grows up, hardness of heart, which usually occurs to protect ourselves from further hurt and disappointment, and feelings of *hopelessness* become the norm. In this place, there is no hope for God to move in the situation, and more than likely, prayer is reduced to praying out of fear or downright begging, or it becomes nonexistent altogether.

At this last stage, the warm, wet, and heavy blanket of *resignation* tightly wraps itself around those who have succumbed. In this place, this type of believer completely gives up, and prayers or thoughts of God's bringing change to the situation are nowhere to be found. Here in this particular circumstance, the believer who gave up now lives in the house that unbelief built, and you and I both know that this is *not* a residence suitable for the sons and daughters of the King!

THE PROCESS OF RESIGNATION AND GIVING UP

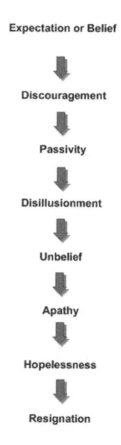

Expectation or Belief

Discouragement

Passivity

Disillusionment

Unbelief

Apathy

Hopelessness

Resignation

This, my friends, is the goal of the enemy; he wants to get us to totally give up and lose all hope in our circumstances. While the Devil does not have a great number of plays in his playbook, the above strategy works beautifully on countless numbers of Christians every day—so why change what isn't broken? Getting believers to the point of unbelief and resignation has got to be one of his greatest strategies, but hear me right now—the Lord is saying that *the time is now*, and He is shining His all-illuminating spotlight on one of the Devil's oldest and most effective strategies.

It Isn't Over, Not by a Long Shot!

Be encouraged. No matter how bad your situation is, there is always hope in God and in Christ Jesus—*always*! God has so much more for His children, and He wants you to know that things are about to *radically* change.

If there are any areas in your life where you have completely given up, even if you are seeing great victory in other areas, then get ready to implement some strategies that promise to give way to victory. God is looking to permanently remove any residue of unbelief, move you further into His kingdom, and give you a brand new base of operation.

I just have one question: Are you ready to embark on a journey that will help take you there? If you are, then buckle up, get excited, and know that God has an amazing plan for you to do just that!

Chapter

A Change of Mind

Now I rejoice, not that you were made sorry, but that your sorrow led to repentance. For you were made sorry in a godly manner, that you might suffer loss from us in nothing. For godly sorrow produces repentance leading to salvation, not to be regretted; but the sorrow of the world produces death. For observe this very thing—that you sorrowed in a godly manner: What diligence it produced in you, what clearing of yourselves, what indignation, what fear, what vehement desire, what zeal, what vindication! In all things you proved yourselves to be clear in this matter. (2 Cor. 7:9–11)

The Beginning of Breakthrough

After God revealed that my mom and I had been through the process of resignation and had bought the lie that things were never going to change with my sister, we knew that we could not stay there any longer. Holy Spirit brought both of us to the sad truth that we had *allowed* my sister and her family to continue to remain in bondage. God reminded us that He gave us the authority and power to bring change to her situation, and up until that point, we had had not exercised anything resembling His authority and power.

My mom had not given up praying for my sister, but her prayers were faithless, fearful, and impotent. If she were to tell it, she would say that her prayers had been reduced to begging and pleading with God to change her daughter's situation. My prayers, on the other hand, were infrequent at best, and at the end of the day, I had already bought the lie that things would never change, so why bother? In some respects, hardness of heart had allowed me to basically give up on her situation, and in my mind, it was all completely justified. Holy Spirit also revealed that when I put the focus on my sister and her behavior, instead of taking this issue before God, it made it much easier to let myself off the hook. At the time, it all made sense, but in retrospect, it was so wrong.

Furthermore, Holy Spirit showed my mom and me the harsh fact that we were walking in judgment of my sister and that we did not resemble any of the Christlike characteristics that He called us to walk in. After our hearts were laid bare, we were truly humbled by this revelation. There was a genuine feeling of godly sorrow, which brought us to tears, as well as the realization that we were partly responsible for the bondage that she and her family were in.

The truth was that without a God encounter, she was *incapable* of coming out of her place of bondage. She was locked in a prison, and no one had come to rescue her. God reminded us that *we* are supposed to be His hands, feet, and mouth in the earth, and He gave us the responsibility to take authority over the ugly circumstances that come our way. If the last statement sounds unfamiliar or even unbelievable, then Hebrews 2:6–8 makes it very clear.

> But one testified in a certain place, saying: "What is man that You are mindful of him, or the son of man that You take care of him? You have made him a little lower than the angels; *You have crowned him with glory and honor, and set him over the works of Your hands. You have put all things in subjection under his feet.*" For in that He put all in subjection under him, He left nothing that is not put under him. But now we do not yet see all things put under him. (emphasis added)

As the above Scripture clearly shows, God gave *us* power and authority over things and situations in the earth; so He was expecting us to stand in the gap for my sister and her family and pray for them until they broke free. My mom and I realized that we had been waiting on God to rescue her, but He called us to partner with Him to do it.

After we had an opportunity to deeply process all of what Holy Spirit had revealed in such a short period of time, all we could do was humbly ask God to forgive us for being so judgmental toward my sister and for basically doing nothing to bring about a change in her dreadful situation. We found ourselves at the place that Paul talked about in 2 Corinthians 7:9: "Now I rejoice, not that you were made sorry, but that your sorrow led to repentance." We repented, which simply means that we stopped going in the direction that we were headed and turned around. We changed the way that we previously thought and actually did something different. We also came to the realization that if we did not make this change of mind when we did, my sister may very well have ended up in a Dumpster somewhere. But, praise God, we were *not* going to allow that outcome!

So What Happened Next?

It was time to put on the big girl boots and the battle gear and get to work! That same day, my mom and I made a pact and said, "Enough is enough!" We agreed that it was time to go into the Enemy's camp, Navy SEAL style, and extract my sister and her family to safely bring them home.

At this point, you might be asking yourself, *What were you girls thinking? What was your strategy?* Honestly, we were not sure what all of this was going to look like, but we knew one thing—our God is an awesome God, and *He*, the great Commander and Chief, was going to be with us on this mission, however it was to go down. After we dried our tears and repented, God so strongly stirred up our spirits to the point that we could barely contain ourselves.

What a kind and faithful God we serve. Very suddenly, God gave us a healthy dose of love and compassion for my sister, and all of those old feelings we had for her were instantly kicked to the curb. Gone were all of the feelings of judgment and any other negative thoughts that may have been lurking around. My mom and I had a whole new lease on the situation, and we could not wait to see what God was going to do. We felt such an outpouring of love and compassion for her that we couldn't wait to go and get her.

Through this process, my mom and I learned that although we had previously not held much hope for my sister, God definitely did not share our thoughts. He radically loves her and was *always* committed to seeing her free, but at the same time He gave us the authority to go get her from her place of bondage. Little did we know at the time, but that one decision would forever change our family's history. My sister was too far in to be able to bring about change for herself, but God wanted us to labor with Him and help bring her out. How amazing it is that we serve a God who *desires* that we labor with Him to affect change in the earth—and labor with God was exactly what we were about to do. Furthermore, we already had the Helper, His Spirit, and He was going to lead the way and show us exactly what to do.

If you have found yourself at the place where you have given up hope in one or more of your circumstances, then be encouraged because what God did for us He will most certainly do for you! If you have given up hope and want to see your circumstances get turned on their ugly heads, then all you have to do is ask Holy Spirit to show you how to move out of that place of unbelief and hopelessness and into partnering with Him. Second, turn your focus away from the person or circumstance that you have given up on and ask Him to show you the role you may have played or did not play in all of this.

As mentioned earlier, keeping the focus on my sister and what she was doing made it easy to let myself off the hook and justify my own behavior and inaction. Over the years, I have learned that if I assign 100 percent of the fault or blame to someone or something else, then I will not be in a good position to see my own contribution to the situation; and as a result, I will not take responsibility for it or do anything about it. This is actually a form of pride, and we know from Scripture that God opposes pride! James 4:6 says that, But He gives a greater grace. Therefore it says, "God is opposed to the proud, but gives grace to the humble." When the Lord showed me my own heart and the role that I actually played, only then was it possible for me to move out of that place of inaction and take a different course of action.

God Is Ready to Move!

The wonderful thing about the grace of God is that if you ask Him to *help you believe* that He can change your situation, then He is more than happy to do so. As I write this, I'm reminded of the story of the demon-possessed boy and how he was not healed by Jesus's disciples. When the father told Jesus about this, He responded by saying that they were a faithless generation, and He basically asked how long He would have to put up with their nonsense. The boy's father then asked Jesus if there was anything that He could do, and Jesus responded, "If? There are no 'ifs' among believers. Anything can happen." No sooner were the words out of His mouth the father cried, "Then I believe. Help me with my doubts!" (Mark 9:23 The Message, or MSG). The point I want to make is that even if you have doubts, God can cause you to break through your situation. You can ask Him to help you in your place of doubt and unbelief, and He most definitely will!

The reason that I can so confidently say that God will help you is because He did it for us, and God is no respecter of persons. Scripture clearly supports this in Acts 10:34–36 (MSG): "God plays no favorites! It makes no difference who you are or where you're from—if you want God and are ready to do as he says, the door is open. The Message he sent to the children of Israel—that through Jesus Christ everything is being put together again—well, he's doing it everywhere, among everyone." Again, there are no favorites.

Finally, once you have allowed God to reveal what's in your heart and have asked forgiveness for the part that you played in your particular circumstance, even if it is inaction, then all you have to do is let Him do the work to repair your heart. You can be assured that God will give you the grace and any other resource you need to successfully combat your situation. You are now ready to receive the prayer strategy that brought about numerous miracles within the days, weeks, months, and years of implementation.

In the next chapter, I will outline this prayer strategy, and it is my belief that if you allow God (through Christ and Holy Spirit) to help you implement this mighty strategy in your life, then you will see incredible breakthrough in those situations that you thought would never change. As a result of the Prayer Pattern, my sister's life has been changed forever, and not only that, but we experienced incredible breakthroughs in our family's lives as a whole. This is why we are sharing *Prayer Pattern.* Be encouraged—*help is on the way!*

Chapter 3

What Exactly Is the Prayer Pattern?

In this manner, therefore, pray: Our Father in heaven, hallowed be Your name. Your kingdom come. Your will be done on earth as it is in heaven. (Matt. 6:9–10)

Let us therefore come boldly to the throne of grace that we may obtain mercy and find grace to help in time of need. (Heb. 4:16)

Then you will call upon Me and go and pray to Me, and I will listen to you. And you will seek Me and find Me, when you search for Me with all your heart. (Jer. 29:12–13)

Be anxious for nothing, but in everything by prayer and supplication, with thanksgiving, let your requests be made known to God; and the peace of God, which surpasses all understanding, will guard your hearts and minds through Christ Jesus. (Phil. 4:6–7)

God's Strategy, Not Ours

First and foremost, the Prayer Pattern is not anything that originated from my mom or me. This is God's strategy, and He spoke it to us through His Holy Spirit. We have full assurance that this was from Him because the strategy that He gave us is in His Word, and it works; within a day of implementing it ourselves, Robert called my mom to tell her, "Whatever you guys are doing, keep it up. I don't know what's going on, but something powerful is happening and I can feel it in my spirit!"

My mom had previously told Robert that we were going to be praying for their whole family, but you know how it goes when people say that they are going to pray for you. First of all, are they just talking or do they really mean it? Second, what are they praying for and to whom are they praying? Are they going to pray one time and forget about it, or are they going to take it seriously and boldly get before God's throne until there is an answer?

The point is that you really don't know, and neither did Robert; but by *the next day*, he knew without a shadow of a doubt that some serious prayer was taking place and that God was on the move.

Before God began to show us His prayer strategy, He pointed out that when He convicts His people of something, as long as we are willing to make the change, He will always give us the strategy to bring about the change that He desires. So combined with our change in heart about my sister's situation and the willingness to do whatever He would lead us to do, God immediately began showing us the strategy for complete and lasting breakthrough—*once and for all!*

Here is what Holy Spirit told my mom and me to do: pray and declare over this situation for ten to fifteen minutes per day, every day—even on holidays and weekends—until further notice. He wanted us to pray and declare together, not by ourselves, and we were to do it daily.

I can see it now—some of your hearts just sank when you read about how we pray because you are already in the practice of praying or declaring over your situations and for much longer periods of time, and maybe you have not seen the changes you thought you'd see. Don't worry, though, because this prayer strategy is probably different than how you are currently praying. Remember—my mom was *regularly* praying for my sister, but she was still firmly in her place of bondage. So what is the difference?

Praying with Power from the Throne Room (The Heavenly Places)!

The difference with this particular prayer strategy is not about us praying from our prayer closet, bedroom, basement, or wherever it is that we pray. This strategy is about praying by visually and imaginatively positioning yourself in the place of the heavens, seated there in the throne room and listening in to the hearts of the Father and the Son, and then allowing Holy Spirit to reveal to you what the Trinity has to say about your specific situation. When you get a sense of what is being said, then you verbally declare that out into the earth. You are to imagine that you're at the throne of God, that Jesus is sitting there at His right hand, and that you are able to listen in on what They are saying about your situation or anything else that they want you to declare into the earth. Additionally, I try to imagine some of the other things that I might see while I am in the throne room, like angels, elders, and creatures. This helps me to really focus when I am praying from the heavenly places.

> Revelation 7:11
> All the angels stood around the throne and the elders
> and the four living creatures, and fell on their faces
> before the throne and worshiped God.

If you are somewhat or even thoroughly confused by the previous paragraph, it's okay. Allow me to provide some Scriptures that may help to clarify things and show you (if you have accepted Jesus Christ as your personal Lord and Savior) what God's Word says about how you are actually positioned in the spirit realm, your inheritance, and the privileges or blessings that we as believers get to access as a result.

Truth Number 1

> "Even when we were dead in trespasses, (He) made
> us alive together with Christ (by grace you have
> been saved), and raised us up together, *and made us*
> *sit together in the heavenly places in Christ Jesus.*" (Eph.
> 2:5–6, emphasis added)

God raised us up with Christ after He ascended into heaven and *made us sit together with Christ* in the heavenly places. This means that although we occupy a physical space here on earth, we also occupy a spiritual space in the heavenly places. So because we are connected to God through Christ and His spirit, we can always operate from this spiritual position and consequently affect things here on the earth. It's the same as being *in* the world but not *of* the world. Your base of spiritual operation is to be the throne room of God and what you establish through prayer and declaration in the throne room will be made manifest on the earth.

Truth Number 2

> In Him also *we have obtained an inheritance,* being
> predestined according to the purpose of Him who
> works all things according to the counsel of His will.
> (Eph. 1:11)

God assures us that we have an inheritance through Christ Jesus. Remember—for you to obtain an inheritance, *someone has to die*! Jesus died, and for those who accept Him as their personal Lord and Savior, there is an inheritance. Jesus is the King of Kings, and His kingdom wealth is beyond imagination; since we are sons and daughters of the living God, *then what He has, we have*! I don't know about you, but I'm taking hold of that truth, and I want every single crumb that He has allotted for me. When my time is up on this earth, I want Him to say that I left *nothing* on His table of provision for my life.

As a side note, you'll find throughout this book that I love to use natural examples to help explain, and consequently aid in understanding, spiritual truths. So imagine that your mega rich uncle passed away and left you an inheritance of $100 million. Nice uncle, huh? Let's just say that you did not know your uncle that well and were unaware that he had left you an inheritance, and for much of your life you struggled with major money problems.

Everyone looking at this case from an outside perspective would say that this was a travesty and a shame. There you were with an account somewhere with your name on it, meaning you had more money than you would know what to do with, and yet, you struggled daily. Why? The simple answer is that you did not have a relationship with your uncle and therefore did not know that you had an inheritance. In this example, you might think that this sounds too farfetched and a bit extreme, but is it? Unfortunately, I've known too many believers with inheritances through Christ who live as though they are in severe poverty and lack.

If you think about a believer who does not have a close relationship with Christ, is not regularly in God's Word, and does not go to church or listen to teachings on God's Word, how on earth is he or she supposed to know about their inheritance in Christ Jesus? One of the most important ways for a believer to learn about their inheritance is to regularly spend time in God's word. Knowing and applying God's truth for our lives is the best way for believers to quickly grow and blossom in the kingdom of God. One thing that I have learned is that this kind of knowledge generally does not come by osmosis. Therefore, part of my goal with this book is to encourage, equip and empower believers so that they know what we have access to in Christ Jesus and how to walk in the fullness of our inheritance on the earth.

Truth Number 3

> Blessed be the God and Father of our Lord Jesus Christ,
> who has blessed us with every spiritual blessing in the
> heavenly places in Christ. (Eph. 1:3)

As a result of our being spiritually seated together with Christ in the heavenly places, *we were blessed* (past tense) with every spiritual blessing; furthermore, the above Scripture shows that these blessings are located *in* the heavenly places and that they are in Christ. So if we are in Christ, then we have access to every spiritual blessing that we would ever need. Are blessings for kicks and giggles or for our entertainment? I think not. They are for the purposes of equipping us to manage every situation we will ever face while we are living this life. I'm pretty sure that when I die and go to heaven, I won't need those blessings because the presence of God alone will be all that I need. So what is the purpose of these blessings? They are for us, and they are to be used here *in the earth*—to take authority over those things that are not in line with God's Word.

Back to the Prayer Pattern

Now that you see through Scripture that it is not fantasy, weird, or unscriptural to pray from the place of the throne room, we can now go back to the next steps of the Prayer Pattern. Once you have imagined that you are in the throne room and you can see yourself seated at the thrones of God and Christ Jesus, ask Holy Spirit to help you hear what is being said around the throne. After that, you are then to *verbally declare* what you are hearing.

Here's a hint on how you know it is Holy Spirit speaking and not you: you will hear an audible voice speaking to you on the inside. You should come to realize that these words are not your thoughts or your words. It may feel like an impression, but make no mistake, it's a clear voice on the inside. You should sense authority in this voice and it should be louder than your own thoughts. It's those things that you might not have, would not have, or could not have thought of on your own. The things that you begin to speak forth will be seamless and require little to no thought or effort of your own. Try not to think about it too much with your natural mind, but allow Holy Spirit to enable you to boldly speak what you hear.

This May Take a While to Fully Understand—It's Okay

Many years ago, I was listening to a well-known prophet by the name of Graham Cooke talk about being in the throne room and being able to listen in and hear what God and Jesus were talking and praying about, keeping in mind that Jesus always lives to make intercession for us. Hebrews 7:25 clearly states, "Therefore He is able also to save forever those who draw near to God through Him, since He always lives to make intercession for them." To be honest, when I first heard this, I thought, *What on earth is this man talking about? How exactly do you propose that I listen in on what They are speaking from the throne room?* I was completely baffled by what he was teaching. But after becoming more acquainted with the person of Holy Spirit, I started to hear His voice much more clearly and I could separate my thoughts from His. Not long after, I started receiving personal words from the Lord and, eventually, words for the body of Christ as a whole. Be encouraged—if I learned to hear God's voice, then *you will as well!*

About four years ago, God invited me to start praying from an entirely different position—not from the position of praying in my basement, praying upward, but he wanted me to imagine that I was in the throne room with Him in Christ and praying downward. He showed me that when I pray from that position, a position of authority and power, I was speaking and decreeing down into the atmosphere, cutting through principalities, powers, and the dark forces of this world, *making them bow their knees to the name of Jesus.* Unfortunately, I did not use this method of prayer with regard to my sister's situation for a long time, and I think that, in part, is why nothing changed. I saw great victories in the areas where I prayed in this manner, so I know that it is an extremely powerful way of praying.

Basically, this is the first part of the Lord's Prayer in action, declaring the things we hear around the throne into the earth, *so that God's will be done on earth exactly as it was declared to us in the heavenly realm.* Let me remind you that God and Christ are seated far above the works of the Enemy, and if we are seated there with Them, then we also are above those evil works because we have authority over them through Christ. I did not make this up; it is fully backed up by Scripture.

> *... which He worked in Christ when He raised Him from the dead and seated Him at His right hand in the heavenly places, far above all principality and power and might and dominion, and every name that is named, not only in this age but also in that which is to come. And He put all things under His feet, and gave Him to be head over all things to the church, which is His body, the fullness of Him who fills all in all.* (Eph. 1:20–23, emphasis added)

Not Your Typical Way of Praying

This is different from much of the prayer that exists in the Christian community today. Many people pray upward, almost from a position of begging. I know because my mom and I used to do that when it came to my sister. But now, when we pray from the throne room, or downward, we are praying from a position of creative power and authority. When we pray upward, from an earthly or natural position, we have to deal with all of the demonic forces above us, and that can be quite daunting for many. Holy Spirit taught us that when it comes to spiritual matters, proper position and alignment are *crucial.* We learned that when we are properly aligned in the spirit, our prayers and declarations are full of power and possess the authority *to break* even the strongest hold of the Enemy. This is the main purpose of this book—to teach people how to pray and stand in a position of proper alignment and thus a position of power and authority that can realize lasting breakthrough, *once and for all!*

The below strategies are to help you understand how to properly utilize the Prayer Pattern. Sample prayers and declarations are provided later in the book so that you can see what this looks like in practical application. Additionally, I declare that God, Holy Spirit, and Christ Himself would cause you to easily enter into His throne room and clearly hear what's being spoken. May you then boldly declare what you hear into the earth so that His will be done on earth *exactly* as He declared it to you in the heavenly places!

Prayer Pattern Strategies

- **Pray together** with one other person (or several more if you can) for ten to fifteen minutes every day, but if there is no one else, then pray out loud by yourself.
- **Imagine** that you are standing at the throne of God and Christ Jesus, even imagining the angels, elders, and creatures that you might see there. ["All the angels stood around the throne and the elders and the four living creatures, and fell on their faces before the throne and worshiped God" (Rev. 7:11).]
- **Listen** to the Holy Spirit as He starts to reveal the hearts of the Father and Christ Jesus. You may get an impression of something, hear a sound that you know is linked to something you want to pray about, see a vision related to your situation, or very clearly hear Him speak what He wants you to speak.
- **Declare** that you come before His throne in the name of Jesus and thank Him that you can be in two places at one time—in the throne room *and* here in the earth.
- **Refer** to God, Christ Jesus, and Holy Spirit in first person (as though you are talking to God in person), not in the third person (like He's not there).
- **Thank God** and Christ that you can simply enter in and be in Their magnificent presence to listen in to what They are declaring around the throne. Thank God for who He is and for who you are in Christ Jesus.
- **Ask Holy Spirit** to tune your spiritual ears to what God and Christ are saying and to clearly speak those things into your heart so that you can declare what you are hearing.
- **Tune in** to what Holy Spirit speaks to you throughout the day. He will give you and your partner (if you have one) specific things to bring into the throne room and declare from His throne of grace. You may even hear something on the news that He says to declare over later.

- **Pray** for those who are dealing with difficult circumstances. Declare over them and be expectant that what you declare for them will come to pass- be bold!
- **Everything you do** must be done from a spiritual position, not out of the flesh or a carnal or religious mind-set. *This whole thing should originate from God's spirit.*
- **Trust Holy Spirit.** Do not overthink things and try to rationalize, minimize, or justify what you think you are hearing; trust that God *wants* to speak to your heart and will very clearly let you know what He wants to declare. Think about it—if He is in the heavenly place and you are seated there with Christ and in Christ, then He will declare His higher thoughts to you. ["For My thoughts are not your thoughts, Nor are your ways My ways," says the Lord. "For as the heavens are higher than the earth, So are My ways higher than your ways, And My thoughts than your thoughts" (Is. 55:8–9). "However, when He, the Spirit of truth, has come, He will guide you into all truth; for He will not speak on His own authority, but whatever He hears He will speak; and He will tell you things to come" (John 16:13.]
- **Don't worry** if you feel like you are stumbling through this. This may be a new pattern of prayer for you, and therefore it may take some time for you to feel comfortable and feel like you are clearly hearing God's voice.
- **Ask for grace** and expect that Holy Spirit will speak to you and let you know how He wants you to pray. ["So I say to you, ask, and it will be given to you; seek, and you will find; knock, and it will be opened to you" (Luke 11:9).]
- **Document** what you are declaring, as well as the fulfillment of those things declared.
- **Be excited** when you see God powerfully moving in your life, and begin looking for other challenging areas in which you can partner with God and declare *life* to those dry areas.
- **Share** what's happening with those whom Holy Spirit highlights to you. When others hear and then see that God is actively involved in your life and that He is causing those

things that you declare in the heavenly places come to pass on earth, then they will be encouraged to co-labor with God as well and become active participants in His kingdom.

- **Tell others** about *Prayer Pattern* and how your life is changing as a result. Encourage them to implement this method of prayer in their lives to help overcome situations and circumstances they may be struggling with.

- **Use free conference-call technology** if you have more than two people on a call. There are many free conference-call services that will help easily facilitate your prayer calls. (Since there now regularly seven to ten of us on our prayer call, we use Uber Conference for our conferencing needs. No PIN is required, and it costs only about ten dollars a month.)

Chapter

Prayer Pattern Disclaimer

Ask, and it will be given to you; seek, and you will find; knock, and it will be opened to you. For everyone who asks receives, and he who seeks finds, and to him who knocks it will be opened. Or what man is there among you who, if his son asks for bread, will give him a stone? Or if he asks for a fish, will he give him a serpent? If you then, being evil, know how to give good gifts to your children, how much more will your Father who is in heaven give good things to those who ask Him! (Matt. 7:7–11)

And whatever we ask we receive from Him, because we keep His commandments and do those things that are pleasing in His sight. (1 John 3:22)

First Things First

There are a few necessary things that must be outlined before we can go any farther. These things are so important that I am devoting an entire chapter to them. Any person reading this book must not conclude that I am peddling some magic potion or offering a quick-fix solution to all of your problems. *Prayer Pattern* is not a book about the ten easy steps to the perfect life or a book about how to quickly and painlessly get through all of your problems. God *always* does His part, but we also play an important role in all of this. Additionally, *Prayer Pattern* is not about ordering or commanding God to do anything. This is about co-laboring with God, declaring what He leads us to declare, and then seeing His will done on earth as it is in heaven.

God Is Not Santa Claus

While the above Scripture in Matthew should deeply encourage every believer, there will always be some believers who take this Scripture out of context and think that *everything* they pray for should be answered exactly the way they prayed. Some go so far as to leave the faith because God has not answered their prayers as expected. God is not Santa Claus or some genie in a bottle who will grant you three wishes if you rub his cute little belly and free him. We serve a holy God that expects His kingdom citizens to walk in the righteousness of Christ, which includes obedience, humility, and the fruits of His spirit outlined in His Word. Fortunately for us, we get to operate in God's grace, and He gives us the tools we need to be able to walk in a way that is pleasing to Him.

> But *the fruit of the Spirit* is love, joy, peace, longsuffering, kindness, goodness, faithfulness, gentleness, self-control. Against such there is no law. *And those who are Christ's* have crucified the flesh with its passions and desires. *If we live in the Spirit, let us also walk in the Spirit.* (Gal. 5:22–25, emphasis added)

Playing Our Part

It is important to note that walking in the Spirit is not about deeds or works. Over the years, I've learned that the more I desire to be about God and His kingdom business, the more I see Him be about my business—whatever that may happen to be. Matthew 6:33 says it best: "But seek first the kingdom of God and His righteousness, and all these things shall be added to you."

"All these things" are all of the things that I need—again, whatever that happens to be. In order to know about the kingdom of God and His righteousness, it is imperative that we live and walk in the Spirit. There is a lot more to this subject; therefore, the subject of walking in the Spirit will be discussed in a separate chapter ("You Are Not Alone—You Have a Helper").

In the last chapter, I provided you with the definition of Prayer Pattern and how it can be applied to your life, but I also want to make it abundantly clear that when it comes to God, He is the author and holder of the plans over your life and the lives of others. Yes, my family has seen powerful results with Prayer Pattern, but God operates in His own time, and He will manifest the things that we declare in the proper time and season. Some things may take longer than others. With that said, you should still be encouraged because I truly believe that we are in a season of acceleration, and many are seeing amazing manifestations of things declared come to pass in short periods of time. Remember—the very day after my mom and I began the Prayer Pattern that God gave us, Robert called to tell my mom to keep up whatever we were doing because he was *seeing* a manifestation of God's power in the situation with my sister.

God Desires to Move on Our Behalf

The point I'm trying to make here is that God definitely expects us to walk according to His spirit and consequently exhibit the fruit of the spirit. However, if there is a sincere change of heart and a desire to surrender our lives to Him, then we can expect for God to move on our behalf. In the beginning stages, my sister was definitely not walking in a way that was pleasing to God; however, my mom and I witnessed Him bring great transformation to her life nonetheless.

My mom and I are fully convinced that it was His amazing grace and great love that brought about these powerful changes. We watched God move in my sister's heart as a result of His love for her; combined with our declarations from the throne room. Together, this enabled her to turn from where she was headed and move into His plans and purposes for her life. Keep in mind that all of this went down *without* our talking to or lecturing her about her behavior. We never said a word to her. We loved on her with the compassion that God gave us and declared from the heavenly places, and God did the rest.

My sister's transformation began occurring within three months, but we saw a change of heart in as little as the first few days and weeks. In your individual circumstances, your prayers and declarations may be answered sooner, but it may also take longer. The keys to the Prayer Pattern are consistency, praying from the knowledge that we are seated with Christ in the heavenly places, faith that God will move on our behalf, and obedience to the things His Spirit leads us to do. Because God is no respecter of persons, I am *more than confident* that He wants to become a more active part in your life and see you become a more active part in His life.

What Prayer Pattern Is Not

- A replacement for intimate time with the Lord
- A replacement for praise and worship time
- Something that can be done in your natural strength or wisdom
- A magic potion or a quick fix for the challenges in your life

The Truth about Grace

God's Word very clearly spells out that He expects His kingdom citizens to walk in a certain way. But what if you say that you have not been walking that way, and quite frankly, you don't know if God is even pleased with you? What if you feel like you don't know who God really is nor the role that Christ is supposed to play in your life? How about if you say that you have no clue who Holy Spirit is or how He is supposed to operate in your life? What if you believe that you have not heard God's voice or ever will for that matter?

All of those are valid concerns, and they apply to many Christians around the world. The good news is that God's grace flows so abundantly that even if you say that *all* of those concerns apply to your life, He is still ready to work on your behalf!

Again, if you have a desire in your heart to grow closer to the Lord, are willing to allow Him to show you the plans and purposes that He has for your life, and are willing to work with Him to bring those plans and purposes to fruition, then I'm declaring that you will be able to step into all of these things. Consider what God's Word says about grace.

Truth Number 1

> For by grace you have been saved through faith, and that not of yourselves; it is the gift of God, not of works, lest anyone should boast. (Eph. 2:8–9)

We can see in this Scripture that grace is a gift of God and is not something that comes from us. There is absolutely nothing we can do to earn God's grace except to believe and have faith in Him and His promises. Even if we are in bad stages in our lives and don't feel that we are worthy of any of God's gifts, we will be saved if we simply receive Christ Jesus as our Savior.

My prayer for those of you who are not so sure about all of this is that, as you read through this book, God will begin to minister to your spirit so as to enable you to walk in the fullness of His gifts and promises.

Truth Number 2

> For the Lord God is a sun and shield; the Lord will give grace and glory; No good thing will He withhold from those who walk uprightly. (Ps. 84:11)

God is our sun and shield and has already given us grace and glory through Christ Jesus. We are the righteousness of God through Christ Jesus, and therefore He withholds no good thing from us. Righteousness can be looked at as being in right standing with God and those who walk uprightly will naturally be in a good position to receive His blessings. Even if we are in the wrong position, His grace and His righteous right hand is powerful enough to move us into proper alignment.

Truth Number 3

> And He said to me, "My grace is sufficient for you, for My strength is made perfect in weakness." Therefore most gladly I will rather boast in my infirmities, that the power of Christ may rest upon me. (2 Cor. 12:9)

God's grace is sufficient for us to handle any and every situation that comes our way, and because His grace is enough, we can expect that any weakness we have will be overshadowed by His perfect strength. If you plan on praying the Prayer Pattern, then allow His strength to carry you through this process until you see the manifestations of the things that you are declaring—knowing that the power of Christ is available to rest upon us.

Prayer Pattern Is Not Just about Us and Our Needs

Although God gave my mom and me the pattern of prayer that He wanted us to pray over our individual circumstances, we soon learned that He wanted us to pray and declare over *far more* than just our own needs.

By the third or fourth day of practicing the Prayer Pattern, Holy Spirit had us declaring over the president of the United States, the city of Detroit, the subjects of major news headlines in other nations, and countless other things that were not even on our radar. Frankly speaking, declaring over situations not directly concerning us is what made things so exciting in the first days and weeks of implementing God's prayer strategy.

For example, when God had us declare life over two well-known celebrities, we knew that it did not originate from us. This is especially true given the fact that these celebrities live an atheistic and, at times, a blasphemous lifestyle, and I personally have a hard time stomaching one of them in particular. When God had my mom and me declare over their lives, it showed us that He cares far more than we could ever process with our natural minds. I was so quick to judge them, but I'm thankful that God demonstrated to us that *despite* their lifestyles, He still very much loves them and desires that they turn to Him.

Now that we are two years into this journey, the excitement has not only increased, but there has been a corresponding manifestation of miracles, signs, and wonders. The word *excitement* does not even come close to adequately describing how we feel about God and the things that He has done in and through us! We can only imagine what things will look like in a year from now, let alone in the years to come. God has shown us through all of this that He is so quick to work on our behalf, and again, I'm confident that He will do the same for you.

Possible Areas of Declaration: Just a Few Examples

Personal

- Encounters with God
- Intimacy with God
- The breaking of strongholds
- Areas of struggle or bondage (addictions, etc.)
- Physical, emotional, or spiritual healing
- Weaknesses
- Guilt and shame
- Unforgiveness
- Purpose in life
- Difficult decisions

Marriage and Family

- Spouse
- Walking together in unity
- Areas of bondage
- Guilt and shame
- Intimacy
- Each child
- Family unity
- Friends and immediate family
- Your church and the body of Christ as a whole

City

- Local government and its leaders
- Local churches (the various denominations and other faiths as well)
- The economy
- The education system
- Cultural issues
- Moral decline and decay
- Police officials
- Local businesses
- Crime-ridden areas
- Restoration

Region
- Your region and other regions

Your nation and other nations
- Government leaders (the president and his cabinet, the senate, congress, the supreme court justices, lobbyists, and etc.)
- National and international issues
- The various Christian denominations and other faiths around the world
- Human trafficking
- Sex trade
- War torn areas
- Genocide
- Disasters and crises
- Cultural issues
- Moral decline and decay
- Religious freedom
- The economy
- Political issues
- Elections

Chapter **5**

The Heavenly Places
and the White House

> But God, who is rich in mercy, because of His great love with which He loved us, even when we were dead in trespasses, made us alive together with Christ (by grace you have been saved), and raised us up together, and made us sit together in the heavenly places in Christ Jesus, that in the ages to come He might show the exceeding riches of His grace in His kindness toward us in Christ Jesus. (Eph. 2:4–7)

> And what is the exceeding greatness of His power toward us who believe, according to the working of His mighty power which He worked in Christ when He raised Him from the dead and seated Him at His right hand in the heavenly places, far above all principality and power and might and dominion, and every name that is named, not only in this age but also in that which is to come. (Eph. 1:19–21)

We Are Seated in the Heavenly Places- For Real!

For many believers, the concept that we are actually seated together with and in Christ in the heavenly places may sound foreign, weird, unbelievable, or downright crazy. However, it is important to establish from Scripture that we are in fact seated with Christ and in Christ in the heavenly places and that the heavenly places have a very real and specific location. The truth is that we as believers get to operate from two dimensions at the same time. In the natural dimension, we live in a body and in the physical world; but spiritually, we get to live in or operate from the heavenly places where we are seated with Christ and in Christ- the spiritual dimension. This is part of the inheritance of every person who accepts Christ as their personal Lord and Savior.

Practically speaking, think about it like this: when circumstances or situations come our way, we usually and sometimes automatically see those circumstances from a natural perspective. Why do we do this? We do this because seeing with our natural eyes is how we normally process things.

Because we are seated with Christ and in Christ in the heavenly places, we get to see those *same* circumstances from God's and Christ's perspective. Consider flying in an airplane at thirty thousand feet and looking far below. What do you see, and how does it appear to you? Most people would answer that the things that they see far below look extremely tiny and may not be visible at all.

The example that I gave you was at thirty thousand feet, but how much higher are the heavenly places? I would imagine that the heavenly places are *significantly,* or infinitely, higher. The next question is, if you are significantly or infinitely higher than thirty thousand feet and you look far below, how much smaller or even invisible would those same things look?

It's all about perspective. Keep in mind that the important thing is not *what* you actually see with your eyes, but *how you view what you see* with your eyes. This is why numerous people can see the same exact thing but somehow interpret that thing very differently. Again, it's all about perspective and how you see the things that you view.

When it comes to viewing your circumstances, from whose perspective and which vantage point are *you* looking? As for me, I've learned that when I view my circumstances from a natural perspective, those circumstances often look very big and intimidating.

On the other hand, when I look at things from God's perspective, then I get to see what He sees and use the resources He gives me to overcome those things. That is how things work in God's kingdom. I elaborate much more on this topic in the chapter titled "Keep Your Eyes Fixed on God."

The Heavenly Places Have a Location

Now that I have established that we are spiritually seated with Christ in the heavenly places, I would like to point out the significance of the location of the heavenly places referenced in the beginning of this chapter. In those Scriptures, we see that Christ is seated at the right hand of the Father *in the heavenly places*. Additionally, the heavenly places have a very specific location. We see that this amazing place is located *far above* every evil force and every name that is named—now and forever more. Conversely, we can also say that *all* of these evil forces are located *far below* the heavenly places.

Here is another natural example to help explain this important spiritual truth. If you were standing on the rooftop of a ten-story building that had no elevators or stairs and there was some huge scary dude down on the ground threatening you, how worried would you be? More than likely, you would not be too afraid of him.

I'm sure your next thought would gravitate toward when you had to come down from that building. Now imagine that you were equipped with a military-grade automatic weapon; how scared would you be then? There would not be an ounce of fear in you because you would know that even when you got down to his level, you would still have the advantage.

As believers, we should have the exact same kind of confidence. We are seated with Christ and in Christ *far above* all of the evil forces—and everything else for that matter. Additionally, we are equipped with the whole armor of God ["Put on the whole armor of God, that you may be able to stand against the wiles of the devil" (Eph. 6:11)], *and* we have the King of the universe right by our side.

This truth alone should cause us to have a much greater degree of confidence when we face circumstances and situations. If our base of operation is the heavenly places, then we should be able to view our circumstances from the standpoint that, as sons and daughters of God, we are well-equipped to fight every battle that comes before us. Furthermore, in the grand scheme of things, those circumstances are really small and insignificant in and of themselves.

The Heavenly Places and the White House

As I began thinking about how to best illustrate the concept of operating from the heavenly places, Holy Spirit provided an excellent natural example that almost anyone can understand. He started speaking to me about the White House in the United States of America. He also spoke about how this place of operation has some very distinct benefits and advantages to all those who live there. As I began thinking about the White House, which is the official residence of the president, and the things that I know to be true about this place, several things came to mind:

- The president was elected and therefore is qualified to live in this place.
- The president of the United States holds the most powerful position in the world.
- Access to the inside of this place is prohibited without an invitation.
- Its physical location is difficult to access.
- Unless someone bombs the place (there are provisions for that as well), an enemy would have an extremely difficult time penetrating this place.
- Everyone in the presidential family has specially trained individuals to protect them.
- Those standing outside the gate who threaten the occupants of the White House will be arrested and thrown in jail if they keep it up.
- The president's children have access to the things of the president while living in the White House.

- Living in the White House affords the president and his family authority, privilege, favor, abundant opportunities, provision, incredible protection, access to information, and countless other benefits.
- There is no lack in this place.
- Those who visit the White House are blessed and honored to be there.
- Laws written or signed in this place (in the Oval Office) take effect in other places, such as the states in which those laws apply.
- The world watches and responds to the things that take place in the White House.

Now, if we go back to thinking about operating from the heavenly places, most of the above points about living in the White House would apply to us as kingdom citizens. This example is obviously not an exhaustive one; however, we can plainly see numerous parallels.

In this natural example, we can easily grasp the concept of the position, authority, protection, benefits, and everything else that goes along with living in the White House. Is it then that much of a leap to believe that, if we also operate from the heavenly places, we would be naturally entitled to all of those benefits, and even far greater things? God and Christ Jesus are far greater than any president has ever been or will be, and the heavenly places are infinitely superior to the White House. So how much more are we, as sons and daughters of the Most High God, entitled to all that He has? I'd say much, much more!

> Blessed be the God and Father of our Lord Jesus Christ, who has blessed us with every spiritual blessing in the heavenly places in Christ... He predestined us to adoption as sons by Jesus Christ to Himself, according to the good pleasure of His will, to the praise of the glory of His grace, by which He made us accepted in the Beloved... In Him also we have obtained an inheritance, being predestined according to the purpose of Him

who works all things according to the counsel of His will. (Eph. 1:3, 5–6, 11)

The President's Children

Imagine the current president's children living in the White House and all the privileges afforded to them. Now imagine that either one of President Obama's teenage daughters decided that she did not want to live there any longer, instead choosing to live on the street, eating out of trash cans and begging for food. It's almost hard to even imagine that happening, but let's continue on anyway. How often would the president go looking for her to tell her how much he loves her and that everything she needs is at the White House? How often would the president plead with her, saying that her behavior is not worthy of a president's daughter and that she should come home? How often would the Secret Service agents monitor her whereabouts and try to convince her that she needs to come home and be with her family? I'm sure it would be quite often—probably even daily.

Too often, I see believers who live life as though they are living on the street or eating out of trash cans. It's almost like there is no concept that all the provisions for everything we need in life is right there in Christ Jesus and is in the heavenly places. Remember—the truth is that we are seated with Christ in the heavenly places and have been blessed with *every* spiritual blessing.

This is not a rebuke, but if we as believers are content with barely getting by, living in lack, and feeling that we are always being defeated, then we are not accessing the things that are available to us. I don't want to oversimplify things, but much of the problem of accessing the blessings in the heavenly places is related to improper position or alignment. We need to be operating from the heavenly places rather than operating from our natural positions.

The Benefits

While the teenage daughter in our example has all of the access and benefits of living in the White House, she does *not* have those benefits when she decides that she would rather live on the street. The point here is that although she has *access* to all of the great benefits of living in her parents' house, unless she is physically living in and agrees to at least try to abide by the rules of the White House, then unfortunately she cannot obtain or possess those things.

After reading this example about the president's daughter, you can easily see how and, more importantly, *why* she would not have access to the provisions of the White House. It's pretty simple—she needs to be *living in the White House* to have easy and abundant access to all that is available to her. Here's the main takeaway: in order to have access to all of the benefits of the heavenly places, we must be spiritually located or positioned *in* the place in which the benefits are derived. So for us as believers, we need to be operating from or positioned in the heavenly places in Christ Jesus so that we can access all of the benefits available to us. This means that we are looking at God when things happen that we do not understand. We are to ask how we should be responding to those things and ask Him to show us what He wants us to see, and more importantly, what He wants us to learn from that situation. There is a purpose for the trials, so it is imperative that we uncover the lessons in the trials.

If we are operating from outside of the heavenly places, then it will be difficult to access the fullness of everything that God has so richly provided for us. Make no mistake—God will use us where we are and will give us what we need in that place, but His goal for us is always to have us *living in fullness*!

The other aspect we are able to see in this example is that the president went looking for the teenage daughter who decided she would be better off on the streets than at home in the White House. The president also sent Secret Service agents to make sure that she was safe and to try to convince her to return to the White House. Although we are talking about the president of the United States and his vast resources, we also know that any good father would employ the same tactics—minus the Secret Service agents, of course. To relate this back to our Father in heaven, He loves us with an infinite love, so how much more would He send out all of the resources of heaven to come and look for us so that we could come to the heavenly places and operate from there?

> For He shall give His angels charge over you, to keep you in all your ways. (Ps. 91:11)

> "What man among you, if he has a hundred sheep and has lost one of them, does not leave the ninety-nine in the open pasture and go after the one which is lost until he finds it? (Luke 15:4)

Whether we were previously operating from the heavenly places and left for whatever reason or we never even knew that we as believers were supposed to be operating from the heavenly places, God is sending out the call for His people to come and spiritually reside there with Him and Christ Jesus.

My prayer for each and every person reading this book is that you would allow all these spiritual truths to deeply penetrate your heart and mind, which will then affect your thoughts, emotions, and actions. I declare that God will stir up your heart so that you will want to go deeper in your relationship with Him and Christ Jesus, as well as learn how to hear and subsequently follow the leading of Holy Spirit.

I pray that God will cause you to believe that you in fact are His son or daughter and that you are seated with Christ Jesus in the heavenly places. Last, I declare that when circumstances come your way, you would immediately seek God as to how you should be viewing those circumstances. May He show you what He sees, and more importantly, may He give you the strategies to navigate those circumstances. You already have victory through Christ, so lead with that truth and realize that you have *everything* you need to obtain that victory. Amen.

Chapter 6

First Things First: You Were Made to Dominate!

Then God said, "Let Us make man in Our image, according to Our likeness; let them have dominion over the fish of the sea, over the birds of the air, and over the cattle, over all the earth and over every creeping thing that creeps on the earth." So God created man in His own image; in the image of God He created him; male and female He created them. Then God blessed them, and God said to them, "Be fruitful and multiply; fill the earth and subdue it; have dominion over the fish of the sea, over the birds of the air, and over every living thing that moves on the earth." (Gen. 1:26–28)

What is man that You are mindful of him, and the son of man that You visit him? You have made him to have dominion over the works of Your hands; You have put all things under his feet. (Ps. 8:4, 6)

For we are His workmanship, created in Christ Jesus for good works, which God prepared beforehand that we should walk in them. (Eph. 2:10)

Domination Right from Creation

M any years ago, when I was studying the creation account in Genesis 1, the first thing that struck me was the line in verse 26 that says, "Let *Us* make man in *Our* image." My initial thought was that *God* created us, so who are the "Us" and "Our" in this text? I later learned that Christ Jesus and Holy Spirit were also there in the beginning and that we were made according to the likeness of God, Christ Jesus, and Holy Spirit. In the very next line of this verse, it says, "let them have dominion," so if I am reading this correctly, the Trinity has dominion in the earth and we were made in their image—ergo, we have the authority to have dominion in the earth as well.

Let's go back to a natural example to illustrate this spiritual truth. If one creates something in the natural, then he or she has ownership over the thing created. That person can do with it whatever he or she pleases, including give it away—and that is exactly what God did.

He created the earth and everything in it and then gave *us*, you and me, *the authority to manage it and have dominion over it.* We even have authority over Satan. When Jesus rose from the grave, He took back the authority that Satan had in the earth, the authority that he got by default when Adam and Eve sinned in the garden. It is a fact that *every* single person who has accepted Christ as his or her personal Lord and Savior not only has authority and dominion in the earth but also *has authority over Satan as well—period*! There is no exception to this truth—*none.*

The above Scripture has tremendous implications, especially since this was an Old Testament writing and we are *now* under the blood covenant of Christ Jesus. As a result of Jesus's sacrifice on the cross, those who have accepted Him as their personal Lord and Savior are now seated with Him in the heavenly places.

> I pray that the eyes of your heart may be enlightened, so that you will know what is the hope of His calling, what are the riches of the glory of His inheritance in the saints, and what is the surpassing greatness of His power toward us who believe. These are in accordance

with the working of the strength of His might which He worked in Christ when He raised Him from the dead and seated Him at His right hand in the heavenly places, far above all principality and power and might and dominion, and every name that is named, not only in this age but also in that which is to come. And He put all things under His feet, and gave Him to be head over all things to the church, which is His body, the fullness of Him who fills all in all. (Eph. 1:18–23)

Furthermore, Hebrews 2:14 (NASB) says, "Because of that sacrifice, we know that through death *He might destroy him who had the power of death, that is, the devil*" (emphasis added). So if Christ now has the power over the devil and we are seated with him in the heavenly places, doesn't that mean that *we also* have authority over the devil? Additionally, Luke 10:19 says, "Behold, I give you the authority to trample on serpents and scorpions, and over all the power of the enemy, and nothing shall by any means hurt you." The Word of God is clear: Jesus gave us authority over all of the power of the Enemy!

The reason I'm focusing on this is because I have encountered far too many Christians who are not living the life of dominion that God created us to have. Consequently, I'm here to remind you that we were made to dominate—and right from the beginning of creation! We were made in the likeness and image of God and Christ Jesus, and therefore, the authority that we exert in our lives should be a reflection of how God exerts His authority. Let's start walking like we are the Devil's master because that is *exactly* how Christ positioned us in this earth. We have authority over the Devil, and it is meant to be enforced!

We Have Dominion over the Works of God's Hands

In Psalm 8:6, we are told that God made us to have dominion over His works. Additionally, that same verse says that He has put everything under our feet. Again, this Old Testament Scripture confirms that we were specifically created to take dominion over the works of God's hands. Additionally, we are *assured* through Jesus Christ that we have the victory when it comes to managing those works: "But thanks be to God, who gives us the victory through our Lord Jesus Christ" (1 Cor. 15:57).

Why would God give us victory? First, Jesus is victorious and we are in Him, so that means we are victorious as well. Also, it is for the purposes of completing our assignments and overcoming our circumstances here in the earth. If this is not made abundantly clear in the previous Scripture, then Romans 8:37—which says, "Yet in all these things we are more than conquerors through Him who loved us"—should bring further clarification. Jesus gave us both the victory and a conquering spirit for the express purposes of overcoming the situations that come before us and expanding His kingdom in the earth.

Too often, many believers are overcome and conquered by their circumstances or by the Enemy. My goal is to remind you through the Scriptures that God made us to have dominion over our circumstances and that we have authority over the devil. We know that God is not the author of evil; however, He will allow us to face difficult circumstances because there is great profit in our trials and tribulations.

James 1:2–4 says, "My brethren, *count it all joy when you fall into various trials,* knowing that the testing of your faith produces patience. But let patience have its perfect work, *that you may be perfect and complete, lacking nothing*" (emphasis added). As you can see from this Scripture, it is not about *if* you will face trials, it's *when* you will face those trials. The good news is that through Christ, we have the victory and are more than conquerors when it comes to every trial we will ever encounter!

Remember What God Did in Our Family

Over the course of thirty years, our family watched my sister's behavior deteriorate to a level that caused us to fear for her life. My sister had accepted Christ as her personal Lord and Savior before she began exhibiting any signs of trouble. Although God had *already* given her the victory as well as a conquering spirit to overcome the problems that would come later, it took decades for the manifestation of victory to take place. Thanks be to God that it did take place!

The day that we received that dreaded phone call about my sister's situation was the day that our lives would be changed forever. There was a mighty flood of grace sent from the throne room, and that amazing grace is what changed everything! It was almost as if God Himself was reassuring and reminding us that He had already given us the victory, as well as the authority, to overcome this circumstance and that it was time for us to enforce it. Our response to God's call and the Prayer Pattern that He gave us enabled us to exercise our God-given authority over this thirty-year problem. Change came *after* we responded to God's call and had the willingness to radically believe that this situation could change once and for all.

My mom and I implemented God's Prayer Pattern two years ago, and we have seen miracles that are too numerous to count. I can honestly say that my sister has been set free from her captivity, and there is not even a hint or suggestion that things will ever go back to the way they were. A year and a half ago, my father and sister— yes, *that* sister—joined my mother and me in our daily prayer time, and the transformation that we have seen in all of us has been utterly astounding. Consider this—the very object of our prayer and declarations has become an *active and vital participant* in our prayer time, and now, we can focus on the other family members who are not yet free and anything else God has us declare into the earth.

We Must Believe!

As I have already illustrated, God's Word very clearly shows that we were made in His image and that we have authority and dominion over the things in the earth. Now, we must *believe* what God wrote in His Word. The purpose of sharing the testimony about my sister is to demonstrate the power of operating from the heavenly places and that God, Christ Jesus, and Holy Spirit are *the power source* that brought about the transformation that my family witnessed.

For some, stories written in God's Word, which were written so long ago, may be a little challenging to believe. However, when I share the testimony of what happened in my family, then this should deeply encourage you to believe that we actually do have authority over the Devil and over our circumstances. Through this powerful testimony, I totally believe that what God did in our family, *He will do in yours*! For there is no partiality with God (Rom. 2:11).

I pray that God encounters you right where you are so that you can come into the full knowledge of the truth of His Word. I declare that you would allow Holy Spirit to minister and witness to your spirit man about how He desires you to enter the fullness of all of the provisions that He has for you.

I declare that what took me years to learn will take you months and that what took me months to learn will take weeks and days for you to learn. I declare that God will cause an acceleration to come upon you so that you will know how you are supposed to be operating in this specific season of your life and that you would enter into *all* of the things that He has planned for you.

May you become a powerful resource for the kingdom of God, and may His influence richly flow through you so that you would bring about true transformation in your entire sphere of influence. Last, I declare that you would say, "Let it be so and may it happen to me according to this word!"

Chapter 7

Victory Is Yours!

But thanks be to God, who gives us the victory through our Lord Jesus Christ. (1 Cor. 15:57)

For the Lord your God is the one who goes with you to fight for you against your enemies to give you the victory. (Duet. 20:4 NIV)

Now thanks be to God who always leads us in triumph in Christ, and through us diffuses the fragrance of His knowledge in every place. (2 Cor. 2:14)

Yet in all these things we are more than conquerors through Him who loved us. (Rom. 8:37)

And we know that all things work together for good to those who love God, to those who are the called according to His purpose. (Rom. 8:28)

What Is Victory, Anyway?

As I was preparing to write this chapter, I started thinking about the definition of the word *victory*. We so commonly use this word that sometimes I think we have lost sight of its *true* power and meaning. The equivalent from the *Thayer's Greek-English Lexicon of the New Testament* of this word is *nikos* which means "victory," but the second definition is "to utterly vanquish." *To vanquish* means "to overcome in battle; subdue completely" or "to defeat in a conflict or contest." So when we say "to utterly vanquish," it means "to totally or completely overcome someone in a battle" or "to defeat them in a conflict or contest."

When I looked up the origin of the Greek word *nikos*, the word I found was *nikē*. Does that word look familiar to you? How about that little shoe company with the swoosh logo? Based on the company that Nike has grown into, do you think that the company's name was casually or haphazardly chosen? I don't think so. I am confident that the leaders knew exactly what they were trying to convey when they named their company. I'd be willing to bet that they talked about the significance of the word *Nikē* and how they wanted their company to represent victory.

I love the meaning of the word, as well as the power of that meaning when it comes to the subject of victory. Let's look at what Paul said in Corinthians 15:57: "But thanks be to God, *who gives us the victory* through our Lord Jesus Christ" (emphasis added). Victory was given to us *through* Jesus Christ as part of our overall inheritance. So why is it that so many Christians walk in everything else but victory? I'm guessing it's because they don't know or realize the power and truth of the gift that they have been given and therefore don't know how to access it. Here is the truth: *we can't access* or *use what we don't know we have.* If we don't know that we possess victory as part of being in Christ, then it will be *impossible* to even think of victory as a viable outcome when facing trials and tribulations.

Victory Enforcers!

My mom recently told me something really powerful. She told me that Holy Spirit was talking to her about the subject of victory and how Christ Jesus won the war over two thousand years ago when He went to the cross, died, rose from the dead, and took His seat at the right hand of God. He then told her that *we are charged with enforcing that victory here on earth.* Wow … we are victory enforcers here on this earth! He then reminded her of the Scripture in Matthew 11:12: "And from the days of John the Baptist until now *the kingdom of heaven suffers violence, and the violent take it by force*" (emphasis added). We must have zero tolerance when it comes to the Enemy trying to take what's ours.

When my mom shared this with me, I was immediately led to look up the word *enforce* to see exactly what it means. I looked it word up on Dictionary.com, and here's what I found:

1. to put or *keep in force; compel obedience* to.
2. to obtain (payment, obedience, etc.) *by force or compulsion.*
3. to *impose* (a course of action) upon a person.
4. to support (a demand, claim, etc.) *by force.*
5. to impress or *urge* (an argument, contention, etc.) *forcibly; lay stress upon.*

When I recalled what Holy Spirit said to my mom—"You are charged with enforcing Christ's victory here on earth"—I realized that all of the various definitions of the word *enforce* involve force, compulsion, obtaining something by force, imposing, urging, laying stress upon, and—oh yeah—more force! All of these words contain an element of the violence that was described in Matthew 11:12, which said that "... the kingdom of God suffers violence, but the violent are to take the kingdom by force." This means that we cannot be passive, casual, nonchalant, lackadaisical, lazy, careless, idle, reckless, forgetful, or anything else when it comes to taking the kingdom and enforcing Christ's victory here on earth.

What is rightfully ours belongs to us, but we also have an enemy who is going to do whatever he can to keep us from obtaining that victory. We must not allow that to happen under any circumstance! Remember—we get to *utterly vanquish* the Devil every time he comes our way!

After Holy Spirit revealed this to my mom, she then thought about a car commercial that perfectly illustrated this important point. In this commercial, a younger brother has a toy, and his older brother comes in, takes it, and says, "That's mine!" When they are a little older, the older brother takes a handheld game and says, "That's mine!" In a third incident, that same brother takes the younger one's personal stereo and says, "That's mine!" Years later, when the brothers are much older, the older brother is walking around the younger brother's really sweet car and then tries to open the car door. The younger brother locks the door with his remote and then proceeds to say, "That's mine, Kyle!"

After Mom thought about how this relates to us, Holy Spirit then told her that we are to have no mercy when it comes to the Enemy trying to take what rightfully belongs to us. We are to lock him out and tell him, "That's mine, Devil!" So if we are experiencing an attack on our health, then we can boldly declare by Jesus's stripes, "That healing is mine, Devil." That declaration comes right out of Isaiah 53:5: "But He was wounded for our transgressions, He was bruised for our iniquities; the chastisement for our peace was upon Him, and by His stripes we are healed."

If you are feeling anxiety and fear come over you when a circumstance comes your way, then you get to say, "The peace of Christ is mine, Devil!" This same Scripture says that Jesus was chastised *for our peace,* so that means that when fear, anxiety, and worry try to come our way, we have to *take hold* of the peace that Christ gave us and *reject* those negative feelings. This works in any other area where the enemy is trying to take or get you to let go of what's rightfully yours.

According to Ephesians 6:17, one of our biggest weapons is the sword of the Spirit, *which is the Word of God.* When we boldly declare God's Word, Holy Spirit, who is the power behind that Word, causes it to be wielded like a sword and cause massive damage to the forces of darkness. It's only when we *come* into this knowledge and then *operate* in this knowledge that we can even talk about the victory that was promised to us through Christ Jesus.

When we have the Word sown up on the inside of us, which is exactly what happens when we are regularly in the Word and live what the Word says, then we are in a perfect position to enforce our promised victory in *every situation* that comes before us. This is not to say that we are not going to experience the hurt and pain that comes along with some trials and tribulations, but we do have the promise of Christ's peace.

Overcomers!

Some people may think that when we accept Jesus as our personal Lord and Savior that we will be free from problems and that life will be a bed of roses. Obviously not everyone believes this, but I think enough people believe deep down that if God is in our lives, then He should keep us from all of the evil things that come our way.

The truth is that we live in a fallen world. Jesus Himself said in Matthew 16:33, "I have told you these things, so that in me you may have peace. In this world you will have trouble. But take heart! I have overcome the world." I can draw from this Scripture that since I am in Christ, I *will* have peace when trouble comes. Furthermore, I can even take heart and have encouragement *because* Christ has overcome the world. Wow—that is a powerful truth right there! Let's take it one step further. Because Christ in is me and I am in Him, *I am an overcomer* as well.

This truth is also backed up by another super powerful Scripture in 1 John 4:4, which says, "You are of God, little children, *and have overcome them, because He who is in you is greater than he who is in the world*" (emphasis added). With all of these mega powerful promises about our victory in Christ, we should *never* be afraid of the Enemy or doubt that God has our back in every single situation that comes our way. This is not an arrogant or presumptuous statement; this is a kingdom truth, and we get to take it at face value at all times and in all situations.

Let me ask you a question. Would you be afraid if you were walking down a dark and scary alley with a seven-foot-five armed man walking by your side? I would hope that even the smallest and seemingly weakest people would say that they would not have an ounce of fear. Why would you not be afraid? You would not be afraid because you would know that someone had your back and that he could protect you. While it would be nice to have that big man protect you everywhere you went, most of us do not have that luxury. The good news is that we have the creator of the universe living on the inside of us and He is greater than *any* force that is in the world—visible or invisible!

It'll All Work Out—That's a Promise!

Now that you are all pumped up about having the victory in Christ, I have to now deflate some of that air and talk about how we need to be positioned when messed-up situations come our way. Remember—Jesus said that we *will* have trouble in this world, so we should not allow those troubles to cause us to forget the promise of victory that we already have. If we first trust that God will never leave us or forsake us and that He made us to be more than conquerors, then we should begin processing these troubles differently. James 1:2–4 says, "My brethren, *count it all joy when you fall into various trials,* knowing that the testing of your faith produces patience. But let patience have its perfect work, *that you may be perfect and complete, lacking nothing*" (emphasis added).

So if I read this correctly, I get to count it all joy when these troubles come because there is a promise that when my faith is tested, then patience is produced. Another element that I see from this is that *trials* in this verse are the same thing as the *testing of our faith.* So we have a choice—we can look at our trials as opportunities to say "Woe is me" or we can look at them as opportunities for God to mature us in the things of Christ. As powerful as we may think the Devil is, he is not powerful enough to *force or make us choose to be* hopeless in our trials and tribulations. That is a choice that only *we* have the power to make. No one else on this earth can make us choose to not be victorious. James said that we are more than conquerors, so we are the ones who get to decide if we are going to believe it and if we are going to lay hold of that truth and apply it in our own lives. I'm choosing to be more than a conqueror, and I believe that you will too.

Now that we've established that we get to choose how we will move through the trials and tribulations that come our way, I want to focus on the assurance and the comfort we should have while going through those really difficult times. When I read Romans 8:28, which says, "And we know that *all things work together for good* to those who love God, to those who are the called according to His purpose," I did not notice an asterisk over "all things," indicating "everything but *your* horrible situation." No, it says *all things* work together for good to those who love God. Let's look at some examples of "all things."

- Cancer and other wicked diseases
- Divorce
- Death of someone close
- Loss of a job
- Rape or brutality
- Shame
- Depression
- Addictions
- Failure
- Tragedy
- Victimization of any kind
- Accidents or injuries
- Persecution of any kind
- Homelessness
- Civil unrest and war
- Anything else you can think of

Regardless of how bad a situation might be, God's Word says that it will all work out for good for those who love Him and who are called according to His purpose. So what does that look like? Two years ago, someone we knew had a young son who was diagnosed with a very rare form of brain cancer. Their whole church family rallied behind them in faith, and they stood with the absolute assurance that their son would be healed. The eight or so months during which he received chemotherapy through ports in his chest and skull were not easy, but they always walked in an overall confidence that he would be healed, which sent a powerful message to everyone they met.

By the end of that year, their son received a clean bill of health; no trace of cancer was found anywhere in his body. Everyone who was involved with them was overjoyed by this news. But as wonderful as it was that our friend's son was cleared of cancer, God said that He works all things together for good. Maybe that word *good* should have been replaced with the word *great* because that is exactly what God did in their situation. This same family, along with their children, received an all-expenses-paid trip to the other side of the world as a gift, which was a fulfillment of their son's dream when he had cancer.

If you did not know that this boy had cancer, you would never know that he had been through the most difficult trial of his and his family's lives. I would say that God most definitely worked everything out to their good—and then some. Not only that, but they have experienced countless other miracles that God did on their family's behalf during their son's cancer treatment and afterward. God was not slow in fulfilling His Word, and everyone who knows about their story has been incredibly blessed.

My prayer and declaration is that when you face your own trials and tribulations, you would look at them in a brand new way. May you go into trials with the stance and the expectation of the victory that we are promised in Scripture, and I declare that Holy Spirit would show you how to proceed with knowledge, wisdom, and understanding.

May the Lord give you the confidence that *He* will work all things for the good because you love Him and are called according to His purpose. I declare that you would co-labor with God and Christ in the heavenly places and release all of the provisions of heaven to bring the result that God desires to bring in your specific situation.

May peace overtake you when fearful things come your way, and may that peace, which surpasses all understanding, be released to everyone that you encounter. I declare that your tests become powerful testimonies so that others will see what God did and then desire to come into the knowledge of His goodness and kindness. You are a *victory enforcer,* and I declare that you would *boldly and violently* enforce Christ's victory here on the earth in the name of Jesus! Amen.

Chapter *8*

You Are Not Alone—
You Have a Helper!

And I will pray the Father, and He will give you another Helper, that He may abide with you forever—the Spirit of truth, whom the world cannot receive, because it neither sees Him nor knows Him; but you know Him, for He dwells with you and will be in you. (John 14:16–17)

However, when He, the Spirit of truth, has come, He will guide you into all truth; for He will not speak on His own authority, but whatever He hears He will speak; and He will tell you things to come. He will glorify Me, for He will take of what is Mine and declare it to you. All things that the Father has are Mine. Therefore I said that He will take of Mine and declare it to you. (John 16:13–15)

Nevertheless when one turns to the Lord, the veil is taken away. Now the Lord is the Spirit; and where the Spirit of the Lord is, there is liberty. (2 Cor. 3:16–17)

But as it is written: "Eye has not seen, nor ear heard, nor have entered into the heart of man the things which God has prepared for those who love Him." But

God has revealed them to us through His Spirit. For the Spirit searches all things, yes, the deep things of God. For what man knows the things of a man except the spirit of the man which is in him? Even so no one knows the things of God except the Spirit of God. Now we have received, not the spirit of the world, but the Spirit who is from God, that we might know the things that have been freely given to us by God. (1 Cor. 2:9–12)

Who Is He and What Does He Do?

Four Truths about the Helper, Holy Spirit

Truth Number 1: Jesus promised to send another Helper before He left the earth.

> And I will pray the Father, and He will give you another Helper, that He may abide with you forever. (John 14:16–17)

In John 14 of the *New King James Version*, Jesus is talking to His disciples. He promises that He will send another Helper and that this Helper will abide with us forever. Interestingly, the King James Version uses the word *Comforter* in place of the word *Helper*, but they have the same exact meaning in Strong's Concordance with Hebrew and Greek Lexicon. Depending on the Bible version, *comforter* and *helper* are used interchangeably, but on the surface, you might think that each word has a different meaning, and thus, a different function. It's so amazing that we serve a God who knew that we would need help in this world and would need to be comforted as well. Holy Spirit provides both of those things, but He is so much more than that—much, much more!

As I began meditating on all of this, I asked myself, *What exactly is a helper?* When I looked it up on Dictionary.com, I found that a helper is "a person or thing that helps or gives assistance, support, etc." While this is a good definition, to me it lacks depth. When I looked up the word up in the Greek language, it provided a much richer and more robust meaning, and thus a far better understanding of the term. *Helper* in the *Vine's Expository Dictionary* (Corresponding with the Strong's definition # G3875) is *paraklētos* (pronounced pa-ra'-klay-tas), and it means the following:

I. *summoned*, called to one's side, esp. *called to one's aid*
   a. *one who pleads another's cause before a judge*, a pleader, counsel for defense, legal assistant, an *advocate*
   b. one who pleads another's cause with one, *an intercessor*
   c. in the widest sense, *a helper*, aider, assistant
        i. of the Holy Spirit destined to take the place of Christ with the apostles (after his ascension to the Father), *to lead them to a deeper knowledge of the gospel truth, and give them divine strength needed to enable them to undergo trials and persecutions* on behalf of the divine kingdom

Let's dissect this for a minute. Jesus called the Holy Spirit to our side *and* to our aid. Holy Spirit also pleads our cause before the Father as a counsel for defense or a legal assistant. We are now talking about legal matters, which make complete sense if we look at the fact that we are operating in the kingdom of God (a form of government). He is the mighty King, and Jesus is the King of Kings and Lord of Lords. God is also known as the righteous judge.

> Let the heavens declare His righteousness for God Himself is Judge. (Ps. 50:6)

> For the Lord is our Judge, the Lord is our Lawgiver, the Lord is our King; He will save us. (Is. 33:22)

> Finally, there is laid up for me the crown of righteousness, which the Lord, the righteous Judge, will give to me on that Day, and not to me only but also to all who have loved His appearing. (2 Tim. 4:8)

Since there is a Judge, then we need someone who can appear before Him on our behalf. Although we serve a loving, kind and compassionate God, we must never lose sight of the truth that He is also a righteous and Holy Judge; One who happens to be our Lord and Lawgiver as well. There is an element of reverential fear and awe that we should have when we appear before Him—never a casual or familiar approach. Holy Spirit is the One who represents us before the Father, but there is another role that He plays in terms of communicating what's on the Father's heart. Without Holy Spirit, we have no way of knowing what God and Christ Jesus would speak to us in any given situation. We are blessed beyond measure that we serve a God who gives us His spirit so that we will know His will, what He wants us to do, how He wants us to respond, how we should pray, and so much more. There are several Scriptures that verify this truth.

> However, when He, the Spirit of truth, has come, He will guide you into all truth; for He will not speak on His own authority, *but whatever He hears He will speak;* and He will tell you things to come. He will glorify Me, for *He will take of what is Mine and declare it to you.* All things that the Father has are Mine. Therefore I said that He will take of Mine and declare it to you. (John 16:13–15, emphasis added)

> But God has revealed them to us through His Spirit. For the Spirit searches all things, yes, the deep things of God. (1 Cor. 2:10)

> But the Helper, the Holy Spirit, whom the Father will send in My name, He will teach you all things, and bring to your remembrance all things that I (Jesus) said to you. (John 14:26)

Holy Spirit pleads our cases with God and tells us what's on His heart, but He also intercedes on our behalf. We know from Romans 8:26–27: "Likewise the *Spirit also helps in our weaknesses.* For we do not know what we should pray for as we ought, *but the Spirit Himself makes intercession for us* with groanings which cannot be uttered. Now He who searches the hearts knows what the mind of the Spirit is, *because He makes intercession for the saints according to the will of God*" (emphasis added). It's truly amazing that Holy Spirit helps us when we don't know what we should pray. Have you ever been in a situation and honestly did not have the first clue as to how to pray? I can't tell you how many times that has happened to me, and I was so thankful that I knew that Holy Spirit was interceding on my behalf. The truth is that it did not matter that I did not know how to pray; He helped me anyway—after all, He is the Helper.

Are you starting to have a better understanding of Holy Spirit after reading all of these powerful Scriptures? If you do not have a relationship with Holy Spirit, our Helper, then you may want to put this book down right this minute and ask Him to come into your heart! You could say something like this:

> Holy Spirit, I want you in my life, and I want to intimately know you. I thank you that I already have asked Jesus in my heart (if you are saved), but right now I ask you to make His presence real to me and I want you to make Yourself real to me as well. I want an encounter with You, and I want You to be my Helper. I declare that You would reveal Christ and His kingdom in a fresh way. Holy Spirit, help me understand Your plans and purposes for my life and help me to live the life that God wrote for me before the foundation of the earth. Thank You for revealing Yourself to me today and I can't wait to see what happens next. In Jesus's name. Amen.

Those who have Holy Spirit in their lives know the incredible power of what that means and could never even think about living this life without Him. Personally, if Holy Spirit were to depart from my life and I had to go it on my own, take me out right now because life is not even worth living! I'm serious—I cannot imagine going through this crazy world without Holy Spirit living on the inside of me. What I said might sound a little melodramatic, but that is how much I cherish and appreciate Holy Spirit's being in my life and my being in His life. If you can't connect with this statement, I believe that you will—and soon!

Truth Number 2: The spirit of God (Holy Spirit) dwells in you.

> The Spirit of truth, whom the world cannot receive, because it neither sees Him nor knows Him; but you know Him, for He dwells with you and will be in you. (John 14:17)

Jesus said that we would know the Spirit of Truth and He would dwell with us and would be in us. What's interesting is that in verse 6 of this same chapter, Jesus introduces Himself as the way, the truth, and the life and says that no one can come to the Father except through Him. What strikes me is that *Jesus* said that *He* was the way, *the truth*, and the life and that the *Spirit of truth* would dwell with us and would be in us. So if I discern this correctly, Jesus's Spirit, who *is* the truth, would come and live with us; and not only that, He would be our Helper, and that Helper is the Holy Spirit. Holy Spirit is the Spirit of Christ, and when we accept Jesus as our Lord and Savior, then we automatically receive His Spirit, who comes and lives on the inside of us. John 14:23 says, "Jesus answered and said to him, 'If anyone loves Me, he will keep My word; and My Father will love him, and we will come to him and make Our home with him.'". Wow—God and Christ Jesus have made their home on the inside of us. When you ponder this, you realize that it is no small matter!

As a result of Jesus's fulfilling His mission here on earth, being resurrected, and taking His seat at the right hand of the Father, we got to reclaim all the authority and power that we lost when Adam and Eve sinned. *Now*, we have the Spirit of God living on the inside of us, which allows us to operate on the earth with the tremendous authority and power of God and Christ. We *never* have to shrink back from the Enemy, our circumstances, our past, our failures, our lack, our fears, or anything else that would try to stop us from entering the fullness that God and Christ intended for us.

Truth Number 3: The Spirit will guide you into *all* truth.

> However, when He, the Spirit of truth, has come, He will guide you into all truth; for He will not speak on His own authority, but whatever He hears He will speak; and He will tell you things to come. He will glorify Me, for He will take of what is Mine and declare it to you. All things that the Father has are Mine. Therefore I said that He will take of Mine and declare it to you. (John 16:13–15)

This may be one of the more powerful Scriptures as it relates to Holy Spirit. Verse 14 says that Holy Spirit will guide us into *all truth*—not some of the truth, a little bit of the truth, or almost all of the truth, but all of the truth. Have you ever been made aware of the details of a scam and how the scam artist runs the scam? So what would happen if one of your best friends told you that she just invested ten thousand dollars in this really great opportunity, but as soon as you heard the details of it, you realized that it was the exact scam that you had heard about?

How eager would you be to jump in and take advantage of that opportunity? Now I'm not the sharpest tack in the box, but I'd be willing to bet that you'd run from it like it was the plague and try to take your friend with you! Why? *Because you already know the truth,* and it is impossible to be deceived or scammed when you already possess the knowledge of the truth.

Since Holy Spirit guides us into all truth, we do not have to worry or have fear of being deceived. I've heard it said before that some Christians believe that the Devil has more power to deceive them than the Holy Spirit has power to lead them into truth and protect them from the lies of the Enemy. If we are going to live this Christian life to the fullest, then we must have the faith that Holy Spirit will always lead us into all truth in all situations.

I have never had a time when I have asked Holy Spirit about what was really going on in a given situation that He did not tell me what I needed to know—those things that I could not see below the surface. This is not to say that you will know everything at all times, but you'll know what you need to know at the given time, and He will make sure that you walk in the spirit of truth and not in a spirit of error.

Jesus said that He is the truth and that His Spirit will take of what is His and declare it to us. Since He *is* the Truth, there could never be any type of lie that could come from Him. Therefore, what Holy Spirit declares to you comes from Him, and you can be fully assured that it is the absolute truth. Now when it comes to the Enemy, *he* is a stone-cold liar and can do nothing else but lie! There is not an ounce of truth that exists in him. Remember—he is the father of lies; lying is his native tongue. So just like English is my native tongue, lying is his!

Here is why I am making the comparison. If you start to feel condemned, accused, guilty, bad about yourself, or anything else that would make you shrink back from God's truth, then chances are that the Devil is chirping in your ear and wants you to believe his lies. Also, if you are hearing and believing things that do not line up with God's Word, His truth, then that is another form of deception. Please allow Holy Spirit to minister the truth to those of who you are in Christ Jesus and allow Him to help you cut off all the channels through which the Enemy has been lying to you.

Truth Number 4: The Spirit brings liberty—freedom.

> Nevertheless when one turns to the Lord, the veil is taken away. Now the Lord is the Spirit; and where the Spirit of the Lord is, there is liberty. (2 Cor. 3:16–17)

Here is another great scriptural truth about Holy Spirit. This verse says that where the spirit of the Lord is, there is liberty. Did you catch that? If the "where" of the Spirit is inside you and me and *wherever* He is, there is liberty, then you and I have been liberated! Holy Spirit is so cool because He can do anything and everything, and He lives in you and me. Wow! Not only that, *we get to bring liberty to those in our respective spheres of influence.* This is not a fantasy or wishful thinking, either. Isaiah 61:1 powerfully illustrates this important and liberating truth: "The Spirit of the Lord God is upon Me, because the Lord has anointed Me to preach good tidings to the poor; *He has sent Me* to heal the brokenhearted, *to proclaim liberty to the captives,* and the opening of the prison to those who are bound" (emphasis added).

Again, the Spirit of the Lord is in us, and therefore we get to bring freedom to those around us. This is how God's kingdom is established in the earth; it's by our visibly demonstrating freedom in ourselves and in our circumstances through Holy Spirit. Thus we get to re-present and model the Gospel instead of just talk about and lecture it. When we demonstrate this freedom in our own lives, it brings about a natural curiosity from others and then a desire to learn how we are able to live the way we live. Jesus walked with authority and power because of who dwelled on the inside of Him. His Spirit now dwells on the inside of us, which should cause others to stop and take note that there is something different about us.

Unfortunately, too many Christians do not live lives that cause others to be curious or want what they have, because they look and act like everyone else in the world. Let's determine to live life through the Spirit, because when we do, others will *naturally* be drawn to God's Spirit on the inside of us. When our lives look more like Christ's life did when He walked the earth, we will begin to experience the miracles, signs, and wonders that He experienced, as well as the magnetic attraction that caused others to want to be around Him.

Let's take a look at the meaning of *liberty* as shown on Dictionary.com:

1. Freedom from *arbitrary* (having unlimited power; uncontrolled or unrestricted by law) or *despotic* (autocratic, tyrannical) *government* or control.
2. Freedom from external or foreign rule; independence.
3. Freedom from control, interference, obligation, restriction, hampering conditions, etc.; power or right of doing, thinking, speaking, etc., according to choice.
4. Freedom from captivity, confinement, or physical restraint.

This definition is so powerful and accurate that there is no need to look at it in the Greek to obtain a fuller meaning. When Holy Spirit is living on the inside of us, then we are essentially *free* from the following:

- Tyrannical governments and external and foreign rule, which may be operating in your country depending on where you live
- Control and interference, which the Enemy loves to exert over believers
- Those hampering conditions, known as our circumstances, that can hold us back and hinder us from doing God's will for our lives
- Captivity, which is known as slavery, which by the way does not have to be physical slavery. Many believers are enslaved by fear of so many things.

This last point is so important because Romans 8:14–15 (NASB) says, "For all who are being *led by the Spirit of God, these are sons of God. For you have not received a spirit of slavery leading to fear again,* but you have received a spirit of adoption as sons by which we cry out, 'Abba! Father!'" (emphasis added). This implies that *before* being led by the Spirit of God, we were slaves and we were in fear. But now, we are adopted and we get to call our God Father! I'm beyond grateful that you and I get to call ourselves sons and daughters of the living God and that we have such an amazing, kind, generous, and loving Father. He not only loves us, but He gave us His Spirit to live on the inside of us, to lead and be our guide in this life, and to reveal Christ to us each and every day. What an amazing and priceless gift we have!

No matter what is going on in this crazy world, no matter what transpires within governments, no matter what is happening in the culture, and no matter how much the Devil tries to get us to move away from operating in the Spirit, we are free because we have been *liberated* from all of those things—*period!* There is nothing that we can't do with the Spirit of the God residing and abiding within us. We are free from all of the things that seek to enslave us again, and it's time that *all* of the body of Christ come into this revelation knowledge. It's time that we walk like Christ did when He was in the earth and represent Him in such a way that causes *everything* to change in us and around us!

Prayer Pattern: A Work of the Spirit

When I think about how the work of the Spirit brought about the Prayer Pattern and, more importantly, set my sister free, I am amazed beyond measure. Holy Spirit, the Helper, entered this horrible situation and brought about the solution to bring not only change but true transformation. This transformation went far beyond my sister's situation; it impacted my parents' lives, our family relationships, our church life, neighborhoods, other families, international situations, friends' lives, marriages, and my own life! I marvel at all of the miracles that have occurred over the last two years.

Looking at how God's Spirit lives within us makes me realize that we are never without His peace, love, grace, favor, mercy, and all that He is. Just like we can go to a well and draw out water to quench our thirst, we can easily and quickly access Holy Spirit to fill our every need.

The well of living water that is inside of us is sufficient for us as well as for anyone else who is dealing with their own issues. While the Spirit of God is there for our every need, we must not lose sight of His main purpose, which is to reveal Christ to us so that we reflect Him more each day. When that reflection becomes stronger, we can be more successful in pulling down the very resources of heaven, advancing God's kingdom in the earth, and shutting up the forces of darkness that are trying to advance their own kingdom. This is what Christians are called to do. Once we have our own lives and circumstances well under the influence of Holy Spirit, then we will easily be able to do great damage to the efforts of the kingdom of darkness—all while bringing liberty to those who are under its sway.

Speaking of liberty, my sister and our family have been set free from the grip of the Enemy. What looked like an impossible situation has been so utterly turned around that it almost seems inconceivable that it was the way it was. *Now* we know what true freedom looks like.

The object of our initial prayers and declarations has turned into an active participant in our daily prayer calls, and my sister has become a powerful force on these calls. Sometimes I just sit back and remain silent because I am so in awe of the things that Holy Spirit leads her to declare. Only Holy Spirit could have orchestrated such a beautiful and powerful outcome. We know what this situation was when we tried to handle it, so there is no possible explanation for all of this other than Holy Spirit!

Holy Spirit led my mom and me into a journey of truth that caused us to stop buying the lie that things were never going to change. He shed light on the fact that there is *nothing* that is impossible for Him. I'm immediately reminded of Matthew 19:26, which says, "But Jesus looked at them and said to them, '*With men this is impossible, but with God all things are possible.*" My mom and I intimately came to the knowledge of the truth that the "all things" outlined in this verse also included our dark and hopeless-looking family situation. We are now walking in the truth, and we are walking in a level of freedom that we've not experienced before.

Right now, you should be so encouraged. Remember—God is no respecter of persons, and what He does in the lives of some He will do in others. We learned that this process did not happen by osmosis, happenstance, or some stroke of luck. No! My mom and I learned to access Holy Spirit regarding this situation, and we drew from Him to resolve everything *until* it was resolved—*once and for all!* We were thirsty and we went to the well to access the living water, and freely drank.

Let this be a pattern for you to follow so that you too may bring life and liberty to yourself and your circumstances. This can be achieved only *through the power of Holy Spirit*, and when He does a thing, it is *done and done!* Afterward, you can then impact those in your sphere of influence, as well as have great kingdom impact in the earth.

I declare that Holy Spirit would stir up your most holy faith to believe that you would see that all of the promises written in His Word are yes and amen. May He cause you to walk in truth and rid you of any spirit of error that may be operating in your life. May you come into a fuller knowledge that you have a Helper and that He desires to bring you into proper alignment with the Father and His Son. I declare that you would have a joy and an excitement that cannot be extinguished by any circumstance or any devil! Lord, if there is confusion about who You are, then wipe that out in the name of Jesus.

I speak forth clarity and singleness of mind and purpose, peace, joy, grace, abundant resources, wisdom, knowledge, and understanding, as well as the knowledge of the crazy love that You have for Your people. I banish fear, doubt, unbelief, worry, anxiety, depression, hardness of heart, a poverty spirit, and anything else that would prevent us from stepping into a deeper relationship with You.

Lord, bless Your people in all that they do and let what they do be for Your name's sake. In Jesus's mighty name. Amen.

Chapter *9*

Learning to Hear God's Voice

My sheep hear My voice, and I know them, and they
follow Me. (John 10:27)

O earth, earth, earth, Hear the word of the Lord! (Jer.
22:29)

Behold, the former things have come to pass, And new
things I declare; Before they spring forth I tell you of
them." (Is. 42:9)

First Things First: God Is Good!

J esus says in John 10:27, "My sheep hear My voice, and I know them,
and they follow Me." Right away, we see in God's Word that as
believers, we *hear* Jesus's voice; which means that He must speak to
us. This same Scripture says that Jesus knows us, and we follow Him.
In order for us to follow Jesus, we need to first have instructions.
If believers are referred to as sheep, then it stands to reason that
there must be a shepherd. In John 10:11, Jesus states, "I am the good
shepherd," and according to John 10:2–4, "But he who enters by the
door is the shepherd of the sheep. To him the doorkeeper opens, and
the sheep hear his voice; and he calls his own sheep by name and leads
them out. And when he brings out his own sheep, he goes before them;
and the sheep follow him, for they know his voice."

It is important to establish the excellent nature of Christ Jesus as our Shepherd, and from the Scripture references above, the following is well-established:

Jesus is a *good* shepherd ⟶ He *calls His own sheep by name* ⟶ His sheep *hear* his voice ⟶ He leads them out ⟶ He goes before them ⟶ His sheep follow Him and *know* His voice.

The reason that we need to establish Jesus's nature is so that we come to know that we have a *good* shepherd and that He is trustworthy. Not only that, but when He brings us out, He goes before us. If we understand this concept, then when He speaks to us, we can be assured that He will tell us only those things that are good and profitable for us—even if it is something we do not want to hear. It's just like when God led the Israelites into the wilderness after He set them free from the Egyptians. He went before them with a cloud by day and a pillar of fire by night. He did not send them out into the wilderness on their own, nor did He leave them without His guidance. He was right there leading and guiding them every step of the way.

Let's take a look at a natural example that illustrates the opposite of a good parent. Oftentimes, bad parents curse their children and call them everything but their names. These same parents may not be reliable, and as a result, they cannot be trusted to safely lead their children or go before them. When these children get older, some refuse to hear their parents' voices and will not follow the things that they tell them. In this case, even though we might think it's not right for the child to not listen to their parents or follow what they say, we can easily understand *why* they don't.

Conversely and generally speaking, the opposite is true. Good parents will properly lead their children and go before them, and their children will listen to them and follow their instructions. So, if we can understand the concept of a good parent versus a bad parent and how each of their respective children would respond, then we can easily understand that Jesus, being the good shepherd, loves us like a good parent and will only tell us things that lead us into all truth. Consequently, we should be more than happy to listen and follow what He says.

How Do You Know God Is Speaking?

Over the years, I have heard so many believers say that they don't think that they hear from God. Sometimes there is such doubt and confusion surrounding this subject. Actually, I can understand this because, before I intimately knew about the person of Holy Spirit, I was not able to accurately recognize that God was speaking to me. Only after developing an intimate relationship with Holy Spirit was I able to look back in my life and see so many of the places where God had spoken to me over the years. The beautiful thing about Holy Spirit is that even though I did not know who He was, this did not stop Him from speaking to me and guiding me. Fortunately, I hear Him speak all the time now and can confidently say that He leads me into truth, guides me in prayer, confirms what He speaks to me, and does so much more.

I can remember back to the age of sixteen to think of one of the most powerful examples of hearing God's voice and not knowing exactly what, or more accurately, who it was. As I was standing in our upstairs bathroom one day, I very clearly heard an internal voice say, *Go downstairs and get a box of baking soda and put it in the bathroom cabinet.* At first, I was so surprised because it was not as if we used baking soda to brush our teeth—we did not. We used toothpaste. What I heard was so crazy to me, but it somehow prompted me to go downstairs, get a brand-new box of baking soda, and put it in the bathroom anyway.

At that age, I was extremely lazy; the fact that I went down at that moment instead of putting it off until later tells me that this voice conveyed enough of a sense of authority, legitimacy and urgency that I acted with no delay. As I was coming out of that same bathroom the very next day, I looked in my sister's and my bedroom and saw flames coming out of the trash can. It had already ignited several of the countless shiny and highly flammable magazine pages that were taped *all over* our bedroom walls. I said out loud, "Baking soda puts out fires!" What do you know—there was a brand-new box of baking soda waiting for me in the bathroom cabinet right outside of my bedroom! I quickly grabbed the baking soda and started slinging it everywhere, and as a result, I completely put out the fire. The damage was limited to a small portion of one wall.

Back then, I'm not even sure if I recognized that God was the one who had given me that life- and house-saving direction or not, but when I got to intimately know Holy Spirit some twenty-five years later, He let me know that *He* was the one who had told me to go get the baking soda that day. As Holy Spirit began showing me the other times when He had spoken to me, I started to see a pattern emerge. When He revealed how I knew that it was Him and not me speaking, I was somewhat taken aback.

Here's the Test

Most people are conscious of their own thoughts and can recognize their own normal pattern of thinking. However, there are thoughts that enter our minds, and if we are honest, we would have to say that those thoughts are not our own thoughts. Of course, we all have random thoughts that regularly enter our minds, but as Christians, there are some thoughts that are significantly different, much higher, and much more revelatory than thoughts we could ever produce on our own with our natural minds. Holy Spirit revealed to me that it was typically *those thoughts* that were the ones that came from God. Obviously, these thoughts could never contradict the Word of God and are *not* thoughts that bring guilt, shame, or condemnation or cause us to do anything else that would go against the nature of God.

The other test that Holy Spirit gave me was that the thoughts from Him would occur *simultaneously* to other thought processes. Initially, when I had the thought to go downstairs to get the baking soda, I almost wanted to ignore it because it sounded so outlandish and contrary to my normal thought process. However, as I batted these two thoughts around, I decided that it was significant enough for me to do it—even though I did not know at the time it was from God. Proverbs 3:5–6 gives a directive that we are not to lean on our own understanding, but we are to instead trust the Lord. "Trust in the Lord with all your heart, And lean not on your own understanding; In all your ways acknowledge Him, And He shall direct your paths." So even though I did not know that it was God speaking to me, I trusted what I heard. I did not overthink it, and as a result, God directed my path and kept me and my family out of harm's way.

If I had given too much credence to the thought that we did not use baking soda to brush our teeth or that it was ludicrous for me to do what I had heard, then it's possible that I would have talked myself out of obeying what I heard. This would have been a perfect example of me leaning on my own understanding. If you think about it, not following what I heard could have been disastrous and possibly even deadly—literally. If I had to go downstairs and get the baking soda after seeing the fire in my bedroom, I'm positive that, with all of the shiny magazine pages on our walls, the fire would have been much too big for me to put out by the time I got back up there with a box of baking soda—and that's assuming I would have been able to even think of using baking soda to put the fire out. Who knows? Maybe I would have been too shocked at the sight of fire breaking out in my bedroom to have been able to process that kind of thought. At that point, we would have had to call the fire department, and by the time they would have gotten there, there's no telling how much of the house would have been burned.

The point that I am trying to make is that when we hear something that is *contrary to our own thoughts* and yet there is something truthful or powerful about that thought, we need to listen and respond to what's being said. That is not the time to be overthinking, overprocessing, or overanalyzing what we are hearing. I have had too many experiences when I simply listened to the voice of Holy Spirit and followed what He said, and it has always worked out for me. I've even learned that *because* I have operated in trusting God by doing what I perceive He is saying, His grace is sufficient to cover me *even* if I make a mistake.

Why Am I Telling You All of This?

The reason I told you this story is to prompt you to go back in your own life and think about the numerous times when you heard a voice but maybe discounted it because it just didn't seem right. If this applies to you and you've had a practice of discounting God's voice—not knowing that it was Him talking to you all along—then I'd like to encourage you to try something different. From now on, when you hear something that you believe is not your thought or that seems like it requires more of your attention, please just stop and ask Holy Spirit to help you clearly hear what He is saying as well as understand and put into practice what He is saying at that given moment.

Hearing or sensing God's voice through His Holy Spirit is *essential* when it comes to spiritually operating from the throne room. So if you have had a practice of ignoring (intentionally or unintentionally), minimizing, or discounting God's voice, then it may be difficult to believe that you can hear His voice when you pray from the throne room. The good news is that God made a promise about those who hear His voice and follow through with what He is saying in Luke 11:28: "But He said, 'More than that, blessed are those who hear the word of God and keep it!'" Furthermore, God's Word promises that His Holy Spirit will tell us what God says: "However, when He, the Spirit of truth, has come, He will guide you into all truth; for He will not speak on His own authority, but whatever He hears He will speak; and He will tell you things to come" (John 16:13).

Remember that in John 10:2–4 Jesus promises that we will not only *hear* His voice but that we will also follow Him because we *know* His voice. So considering these important Scriptures, it is time to take it to the throne room where we will put all of this into practice. Again, if you are struggling to believe that *you* can hear God's voice, just ask Him to help you clearly hear His voice and give you the confidence that you will not only hear what He and Christ Jesus have to say from the throne but that you will *boldly* declare it forth into the earth. I'm sure that there are several circumstances you are facing right now that need a serious declaration of life, so get excited because those things are about to change *once and for all*!

So What Does This Look Like in the Throne Room?

When my mom and I first began praying from the throne room more than two years ago, we did not know exactly what to expect. The first day of prayer occurred on a snowy Thursday morning, and we entered into the place of the throne room by simply thanking God that we were with Him and Jesus. We thanked Him for allowing us to access His presence through His Holy Spirit. We thanked Him that although we were in our respective places on the earth, we were also seated with Christ and in Christ in the heavenly places. Straightaway, we both started to receive powerful words that we boldly declared into the atmosphere and, more specifically, we were led to speak *to my sister's spirit man*—where he could hear us loud and clear. We declared that all of the chains of bondage were already broken, and we started calling out those godly attributes that we knew God set aside for her.

We prayed for fifteen minutes, but it felt like we had only been speaking for a few minutes. I actually felt like something had physically happened in the atmosphere; it was as a result of the powerful declarations we were making from the heavenly places. My mom and I both knew with great certainty that we had entered into something extremely powerful. No demon in hell was going to be able to stop what had just been released! Robert called my mom a several moments after we hung up and told her that whatever we were doing, please keep it up. He said that he didn't know how to describe it, but he said *something* was happening! How could he have known that we had just prayed? He could not have; however, he felt the power of what had been released.

As we prayed from the throne room on the next day, I heard the word *freedom.* I began declaring freedom into my sister's spirit man and declared that she would begin to hear bells in her spirit as well as in the natural. While I was praying this over her, I also declared that my mother and I would begin to hear bells as well. This is an example of a thought that was not my own, cuz who does that? Even though it sounded a little crazy, we were totally expecting that we would start hearing bells ringing sooner or later. Two days later, and on separate occasions, my mom and I both heard the audible ringing of bells. It went on for a few days and then just stopped. What we felt led to declare in the throne room had manifested just two days later.

God Speaks Through Impressions, Too

The following week during our prayer call, I had a very strong feeling that the Lord was going to quickly restore my sister's life. I sensed that He was breaking over three decades of a bad foundation. But instead of seeing something so huge and insurmountable, I perceived in my spirit that God had blown on it and there was nothing remaining but dust. In my natural mind, I saw something that would have taken a long time to break apart, but with God, *it was already done*; therefore, all we had to do was blow on it. So I blew on it as though I was blowing sawdust off of a table—it was as simple as that. Again, this was not my thought, but it was something that God had already done, so the blowing off of the sawdust was the last part. Guess what? My sister's mind is being renewed and she is blossoming into a beautiful daughter of God, walking powerfully in the plans and purposes that God has for her!

Initially, when you are in the throne room, you may not clearly hear Holy Spirit say anything specific. Don't worry because there are other methods that He will use to communicate with you. You may receive impressions, visions, sounds, mental images, and other perceptions that are not in accordance with your natural mind-set. There are times when you will open your mouth to declare what you perceive, and the next thing you know you will be saying things that are totally new to you. It will almost be like those words bypassed your mind and its thought process altogether. There will be such a sense of awe and excitement because you will *know* that what you declared did not originate from your natural resources. This happens all the time when we pray. Someone will say something, and I will realize that the flow, truth, clarity, authority, and sheer power of what they said is coming straight from God. Again, this is when things get really exciting. We are mouthpieces for God, and we get to say what He and Christ Jesus are declaring around the throne. *Let's do this!*

God Works Fast!

Within a week of our prayer and declarations from the throne room, my mom walked in her house and heard my sister's voice; she was talking to my dad. This sister rarely, if ever, just dropped by. My mom told me that she actually looked different and that her face was "glowing"—she looked so pretty. She was observing *a physical change* in my sister, and we completely attributed it to her inward and outward man responding to the declarations over the last many days. Keep in mind that my mom and I had never said anything to my sister about what she was doing or how we were responding to what we had learned about her behavior. God was the One performing the work, and we were in awe at what we were seeing!

The reason for sharing these accounts with you is to encourage you that God is ready to move in *your* personal situations and circumstances. What He did for us and our family is possible with you and yours. Remember Romans 2:11 (NIV), which says, "For God does not show favoritism." At this point, *no one* is safe from a blessing from God! Although we did not have any expectation of how things were going to go, we knew that *something* was going to happen—so we just went for it and did not think too much more about it.

The Scripture that now comes to mind is Proverbs 3:5–6: "Trust in the Lord with all your heart, and lean not on your own understanding; in all your ways acknowledge Him, and He shall direct your paths." My mom and I simply trusted that the Prayer Pattern, which did not originate with us, was going to help my sister get free. God not only directed our paths in this process but also directed my sister out of her place of bondage and captivity and set her free. Today, my sister is well on her way to becoming totally free, and she has been powerfully praying with my parents, my 92-year-old grandmother, another sister, other family members, two other people from my sister's work, and me every day for the last year and a half. The bottom line is that the original object of our prayer and declaration is now *an active participant* in declaring God's will from the heavenly places.

At this point, you may be wondering what other kinds of things God had us declare from His throne room. Fortunately, I was led from the beginning to document the first ninety days of prayers and declarations. While I know that God, through His Holy Spirit, will give you very specific things to declare into your own situations, I would like to give you a sense of some of the things that He spoke to my mom and me in those first three months. Initially, you may feel led to declare some of these things, especially until you feel like you are clearly hearing His voice. I've only included some of the things we declared, but know that there was also a tremendous amount of praise, thanksgiving, and acknowledgment of the greatness of God that went on—and still continues to this day.

Examples of Declarations

The Physical Man
We declare the following:

- My sister's neuronal pathways and the synapses would come in line with Your Word, God and that her behavior would follow suit.
- Your will would be done in my sister's life.
- There is a cleansing taking place over the sexual immorality that goes back in our family line for many generations. We *will* walk in true holiness and righteousness for the rest of our days.
- The sleep challenges that have been a big part of our family's history would be healed and that Your peace would be upon every single family member.
- That You would clear our minds of the "blah" and fogginess that sometimes seeks to weigh us down as a result of chronic sleep problems.
- We will not return to behaviors of old, and we will put off every remnant of the old man that we used to walk in.

The Spiritual Man
We declare the following:

- Wholeness would invade every area of my sister's life—spiritual, emotional, physical, and every other facet of her life.
- There would be an increase of hunger and thirst for Your Word and the things of Your kingdom within our whole family.

- Double-mindedness would be renounced and it would be replaced with Christlike singleness of focus.
- We have a new ear to hear what You are saying, and what You speak are words of spirit and truth.
- You grant us the grace and courage to step into the things that You called us to do and become the extraordinary people You called us to be. We are supernatural children!
- We have the strength and every provision we need to do what You have called us to do. We pull it down in the name of Jesus because You, Jesus, are in us. We claim this, but more than that, we wear You like a coat, one that goes everywhere we go!
- You, Lord, would witness to our spirit man to speak to us and assure us of our identity in Christ.
- We walk in the assurance and confidence that we are sons and daughters of the Most High God, and we have a family legacy in Christ.
- You are bringing a total and complete spiritual and emotional healing so that we can be the family that you called us to be— strong, powerful, God-fearing, loving, and a people that seek after Your kingdom.
- Rivers of living water are flowing out of us, and we are seeing permanent and everlasting breakthrough. As long as we drink from these rivers of living water, we will always have an abundance of resources at our fingertips to overcome *every situation* before us.

Spiritual Oppression
We declare the following:

- The spirits that have been hanging around for all these years, tormenting and tempting us to move further and further away from our godly roots, would leave at once and release their grip on Your people.
- The Enemy can no longer come in and steal the seeds that are being planted here in the throne room. You are bringing about a divine acceleration and maturation of those seeds,

and causing those seeds to become food for others who come into contact with those carrying the fruit from this great and mighty harvest.

- You are delivering Your people from their awful places of spiritual bondage brought on by the enemy.
- You have already broken through the powerful enemy strongholds, and those barriers will no longer hold Your people back from accomplishing Your every purpose for each of our lives.
- Our song of praise and worship is another powerful strategy that releases mighty weapons, and those weapons break down the walls of the Enemy. Lord, we release these weapons right now, and once released, we declare that they break the back of the Enemy in each area where he is still operating in our lives and in the lives of our families. We revoke his access card on our lives, and we block his access from here on out in the name of Jesus!

Marriage and Family

We declare the following:

- Our family will experience breakthrough in every area of our marriages.
- Any areas of unforgiveness are being broken
- Newness and restoration is infused into all of our relationships.
- God, You are mending relationships within our family, and we are becoming a strong and healthy family, and we are victorious through all of this.
- Restoration and renewal are flowing to those in our family who have been devastated by the Enemy. We declare that those who are still hurting from old wounds would experience total healing. There will be no more hurt and pain associated with those old memories.
- You are aligning all of us to Your standard and not to one another's standards and expectations.

- You are bringing our entire family into alignment and in proper positioning with You. This is not something that we have to strive to obtain but will simply be able to enter into.
- Your lasso is rounding up the other siblings that are still out there. We hear You say that You are bringing them back into the fold. You have left the ninety-nine to go after the one, but You will bring them all in and there will not be one left, in the name of Jesus.
- God said to me, *the lasso is swinging overhead. Can you hear it? It's circling wide and it's made of gold fibers, and it's rounding up all who are lost and wayward, those who you think are too far out from My reach; but know that this rope has no end and it can reach into all areas to grab those on whom My sight is set.*

Sickness and Disease

We declare the following:

- The sickness, disease, and all the other infirmities hanging around our bloodline (on all sides) are broken in the name of Jesus.
- Sickness and disease (stroke, heart disease, future forms of cancer, high blood pressure, and any other named or unnamed sickness), as well as the structures and foundation that they stand on, are cursed from the root.
- Our entire family walks in divine health as a result of the blood of Christ.
- We have total healing by the blood of Jesus and by Your stripes we are healed! We thank You for the provision of healing that You made available for all of Your children.
- Lord, Your Word and decrees have already gone out, and they stand—no matter how bad the circumstances appear to be. We do not have to be dismayed by what we see with our eyes and hear with our ears!
- Families who have become fatigued over the battle of disease and sickness would be rejuvenated with Your hope and press into the healing that is already theirs through the blood of Christ.

Family Bloodlines
We declare the following:

- The disorders in our family's bloodline and the spirits attached to those disorders are cut off in the name of Jesus.
- Our family bloodline is cleansed, and generational curses are broken in the name of Jesus.
- The spirit of rebellion that has been oh so prevalent in our family's bloodline is broken once and for all.
- We actually have a new bloodline and are part of a royal family, and this royal blood is coursing through our veins.
- The fourth generation, which includes all of the grandchildren—those who are here and those who are to come—have a godly seed in them and their fruit will be known from an early age.
- The generational curse of rejection, the feeling of not being good enough, low self-esteem, and the feeling of being different are broken in the name of Jesus!
- You are a generational and family-oriented God, and You deeply care about all of us. We thank You that our strength increases from generation to generation; and we speak increase over every area of our lives.

God, Christ, and His Kingdom
We declare the following:

- God, You are a loving Father, and You especially care for those who don't have anyone special to stand in the gap for or with them.
- As we listen in to Your and Christ's conversation, we become increasingly grateful for all that's being done and continue to thank You for all that is transpiring in our lives right now.
- We will all experience greater measures of Your love and, therefore, walk in greater levels of compassion.
- You are doing a mighty work in our generation, and the "life of Christ" would be in every child born to our future generations.

- You, God, are causing my family to be forerunners, ones that will eventually be able to show others and their families in bondage how to get free. We perceive that You are showing us a pattern that others can grab hold of, and subsequently appropriate in their own lives.
- There would be a series of encounters with You, dreams, visions, and any other method that You would use to speak to us and transform us.
- There is divine acceleration over our family's lives (blood and church families, too), and they will experience the things of Your kingdom much faster than in the previous generations.
- We will always remain in Your presence and be able to hear what You and Christ are saying so that we can always behold and release the fresh revelation You abundantly provide on a second-by-second basis.
- The things that You declare to us in the heavenly spaces will manifest into reality in the earth—in our lives and circumstances.

The Nations

We declare the following:

- The situation with Russia and the Ukraine would be covered by the blood of Jesus, and we declare this over the people and their governments as well.
- Your peace would be over those families who lost loved ones in the Malaysian airliner incident.
- The missing Nigerian girls would be found in the name of Jesus. Thank You that You are watching over them and that no harm shall befall them. Even if we do not understand why all of this happened, we know that You are faithful and Your Word stands. We intercede on behalf of these girls and thank You that they are in Your care.
- There will be an explosion of wisdom, knowledge, and understanding for our leaders, and You have already equipped

them for everything that comes before them. There is nothing too big for them to overcome.

- Your wisdom and leadership would prevail, especially when it comes to decisions made about Israel.

- Your abundant mercy will cause the potential attacks against our nation to be thwarted, and You would continue to protect Your people.

- Great confusion and division will come upon ISIS and their efforts to behead and kill as many Christians as they can get their hands on. We declare that the principality that operates over ISIS and the Middle East would be broken and cut off in the mighty name of Jesus! Let ISIS encounter You, Jesus.

- Your guidance will be over our city leadership, the mayor, and his cabinet. We thank You for Your wisdom and for great strategies as to how to free this city from its bondage of debt. We declare that the citizens will begin to take responsibility for their neighborhoods and the churches.

Chapter 10

Open Your Mouth and Declare!

You will also declare a thing, and it will be established for you; so light will shine on your ways. (Job 22:28)

I will tell you, hear me; what I have seen I will declare. (Job 15:17)

Death and life are in the power of the tongue, and those who love it will eat its fruit. (Prov. 18:21)

You Speak, God Performs the Work

When you read the first two Scriptures in the beginning of this chapter, it's pretty clear that declaring is not some strange or foreign concept. In fact, in Genesis 1:3, God said, or *declared,* "Let there be light," and there was light. Consider Psalm 33:6,9: *"By the word of the Lord the heavens were made,* And all the host of them by the breath of His mouth.... *For He spoke and it was done; He commanded,* and it stood fast" (emphasis added). When the King of the universe says or declares something, it comes into being or it will come into being at a later point in time. We can look to Isaiah 55:11 to see exactly how true this is: "So shall My word be that goes forth from My mouth; it shall not return to Me void, but it shall accomplish what I please, and it shall prosper in the thing for which I sent it." Basically, this Scripture is saying that you can take God's Word to the bank because it is that reliable!

Since we have already established that we are made in the image of God and Christ Jesus, then the same declarative powers that He has, *we have.* Obviously, our words must be aligned with God's words in order for His will to come to pass, but if our spiritual base of operation is from the heavenly places, then we hear His Word and declare what He speaks. When we speak what God speaks, then we should have the full expectation that those words *will* come to pass. Remember—we as believers are God's mouthpieces in the earth, so it is *through us* that His Word and His kingdom are established in the earth.

In Job 22:28, the Word very clearly says that you will also declare a thing, and it will be established for you. This verse states that it will be established *for* you, so *you* are not the one doing the work—*God is.* If we look back in verse 22 of this same chapter, it says, "Please *receive instruction from His mouth* and establish His words in your heart" (NASB, emphasis added). There is a strong connection here, so let's look at the sequence that we can draw from these two verses, plus the verse in Isaiah 55:11.

God speaks His Word to us ⟶ *we receive* instruction from His mouth ⟶ *we establish* His words in our hearts ⟶ *we declare* what He speaks ⟶ *He establishes* what we speak, and His Word *will not return to Him void* ⟶ His Word *shall accomplish* what He pleases ⟶ His Word *will prosper* in the thing for which it was sent.

All of this comes directly out of His Word. This is not something that I am taking out of context or making up. The truth is that God speaks to us, and because we have two natural ears and one big fat spiritual ear, we are sufficiently able to hear exactly what He is saying. It is through the indwelling presence of Holy Spirit that we are able to hear and speak forth what God speaks to us. Once we speak what He speaks, then God goes about the work of performing His Word and causes it to prosper. When you think about it, this really is not a difficult concept.

We can look at another natural example to see a parallel to this spiritual concept. If you received a seed (God's Word), then your job would be to plant, water, and weed the seed (declaring that word);

but everything needed for the seed to produce what it was created to produce is already encapsulated in the seed—by God, of course. God then is the one who causes the seed to come to fruition, not you. Not only does He cause it to prosper, but He can take that one seed and allow it produce many more of its kind. Only God can do that. Last, *we* are the beneficiaries of what God did, and we get to reap the harvest of the things that were sown in previous seasons.

> Then Jesus said, "God's kingdom is *like seed thrown on a field by a man* who then goes to bed and forgets about it. *The seed sprouts and grows*—he has no idea how it happens. *The earth does it all without his help*: first a green stem of grass, then a bud, then the ripened grain. When the grain is fully formed, *he reaps—harvest time!* (Mark 4:26–29 MSG)

There's Power and Authority in Our Words

Although I have used the term sphere of influence a few times thus far, I want to make it clear that your sphere of influence is much broader than you might think. In the natural, you may only have a small sphere of influence, and that's okay. God can use you mightily right where you are. Besides, your pastor, your friends and family most likely cannot impact your sphere the way you can. I am here to let you know that *anywhere* the Lord sends you or has you declare over *is* your sphere of influence. God gave us creative authority and dominion over the earth right out of the gate of creation! Your impact for God's kingdom is no small thing.

We can go right to Genesis 2:19 to see a stunning example of this creative authority at work: "Out of the ground the Lord God formed every beast of the field and every bird of the air, *and brought them to Adam to see what he would call them. And whatever Adam called each living creature, that was its name*" (emphasis added). God created Adam and put him in the garden to tend and keep it—to manage it. Basically, Adam had authority and dominion over the garden, so however Adam saw or called things in the garden, that's what it was and God accepted it as such! I was utterly blown away when God revealed this amazing connection between the dominion and authority that was given to Adam at creation and how *we* are to exercise that same dominion and authority today.

Think about it—God came to Adam to see what Adam would call the things He created. He is looking to do the same with us. When we face circumstances or things that we don't understand, then He is looking to us to see what or how *we* will call those things. Consider these examples:

- "I know God is with me on this, so I will *not* let this situation take me out!"
- "How do you want me to respond to this, God?"
- "I know that I already have the victory, so I am not even going to get all worried and fearful about this."
- "By the eyes of faith, I am going to call those things that are not (those situations that are not the way that they should be) as though they were (manifestation of what's being declared)!"
- "Even though this situation has always been like this, with God on the scene, it is about to change!"
- "I declare that I can do *all things* through Christ who strengthens me!"
- "No weapon formed against me will prosper!"
- "I don't care what the report of the doctor says; I'm going to believe the report of the Lord!"

We must change our confession to align with God's Word before we can expect to see the changes that we envision in our lives. God deeply wants us to move into the place where we declare His Word over our circumstances with great boldness and faith. Remember—*whatever* Adam called each living creature, that was its name; so shall it be with us when we walk accordingly.

Before Adam and Eve sinned, they had an intimate relationship with God, which enabled them to walk in the fullness of their dominion and authority. We have been restored to God *through* Christ Jesus, and therefore, we have the same authority as Him. This is made abundantly clear in 2 Corinthians 5:17–18: "Therefore, if anyone is in Christ, *he is a new creation;* old things have passed away; behold, *all things have become new.* Now all things are of God, *who has reconciled us to Himself through Jesus Christ,* and has given us the ministry of reconciliation" (emphasis added). This restoration means that we also can now have an intimate relationship with God and have the same dominion that He gave to Adam at creation.

So how do we practically apply all of this? Unless you are a scientist, inventor, or someone who regularly creates things, then you are probably not going around and naming things all the time, but you do have your own sphere of influence. You get to create and shape your circumstances with the declared Word of God and by how He sees those things. When you are seated in the heavenly places and listening in on what's being spoken around the throne, then you will hear the strategies and declarations that you are to speak forth over those circumstances. That way, when negative, fearful, or confusing situations arise, you get to speak over those situations and call those things which do not exist as though they did—again, how He sees and calls them! This is exactly what Abraham did when God told him that he would become the father of many nations. His body was as good as dead in the natural, but God gave him a seed of promise and Abraham believed that God was able to do what He promised, and eventually, his son Isaac was born.

Declaring Changes Things—For Real

Last year I attended a Christian conference and heard a testimony that blew my mind. The speaker was talking about this same subject and how she applied the principle of declaring over potential negative situations. She said that no matter how negative the situation was, she had to fully expect and trust God that *He* would bring about the result that she declared. She told a story of how she and her husband were on their way to a family gathering where the family members were, in her words, "crazy and always creating drama." That husband and wife decided that they were not going to participate in the same negative cycle that had gone on for years. They determined that it was time for a change and that they were going to be the change agents to usher in that change.

They declared that there would be peace in the house, that there would be no strife or drama, that the family would come together in unity, and that there would be opportunities to share the things of God with them. When they arrived, there were some initial indications that the same exact nonsense that had gone on for years would repeat itself, but they pressed in and kept declaring the outcome that they had declared in the car ride. Within a very short period of time, everything fell into place, and for the first time, they experienced a wonderful and unifying time together. I'd like to point out that they did not allow those early signals to move them off of their purpose, nor did they give up just because there was some initial pushback.

When we declare forth God's will in the earth, we can expect that the Enemy will rise up to challenge that Word. Think about it—the serpent challenged Eve in the garden by asking her if God *really* told her that she should not eat of every tree of the garden. "Now the serpent was more cunning than any beast of the field which the Lord God had made. And he said to the woman, "Has God indeed said, 'You shall not eat of every tree of the garden'?" In verse 4, the serpent told her that she would "surely not die" if she ate of the trees in the midst of the garden. In verse 1, the serpent questions whether God said what he said, but in verse 4, he straight up lied to her and said that she would not die even though that's *exactly* what God said.

We must keep in mind that the devil is slick and that he will question and challenge everything that God says. He is the father of lies and has been lying since the very beginning; therefore, we can *never* be fooled into thinking anything different. The key is that if we *know* what God's Word says to the point that it has been made flesh on the inside of us and we declare forth what that Word says, then it doesn't matter what the devil says because God's Word stands! Just like that husband and wife did not move off of their declaration, we must also stay on track and continue to declare the truth of God's Word over our situations. My mom and I had to stand in this same manner all the while we were declaring over my sister. If you recognize and even expect that you may face a challenge from the Enemy, then you should not be surprised or caught off guard by any of this but instead press in that much more. Remember—the Devil has *no real authority over you*, and that is the truth! Greater is He (Christ in you) than he (the devil or man) who is in the world.

Are You Speaking Life or Death?

Look at Proverbs 18:21: "Death and life are in the power of the tongue." I want to point out that *we* are the ones who are in control of the words that we speak. You can plainly see from this Scripture that *both* death and life reside in our mouths, and it's the power of the tongue (what we speak) that determines which one is released. Going back to the example above, if that husband and wife had allowed those initial negative signs to influence them and get them off track, I guarantee you that their words would have reflected it. So instead of continuing to declare what they had declared in the car, their mouths would have started speaking things like, "These people are never going to change," "My brother always creates drama," "I hate coming here and spending time with my family," "I don't know what's wrong with these people," and any other death-spewing words that came to mind. And you know what? I bet their weekend would have aligned accordingly. Think about it—what we declare has a tendency to come forth, either for the good or for the bad.

The point that I am trying to make here is that when we declare something, then we must make sure that our words continue to be in alignment and are consistent with our declarations. If we stay on track by not allowing what we see on the surface to distract us, then words of life will powerfully come forth. Conversely, if we are dismayed by what we see with our eyes and hear with our ears, then we will speak forth negative words that will produce death. The bottom line is that *we, not the Devil*, have 100 percent control over what we speak forth, and the words that we speak must be in alignment with our declarations. One of the goals of this book is to get you to open up your mouth and declare over your circumstances—speaking what God says to you about that situation. But I also want to remind you that you get to choose whether you will speak forth life or whether you will spew out words of death. The choice is yours, but I declare that you will choose life—so please be careful when talking about your circumstances.

Be Encouraged—The Time to Declare Is Now!

Earlier this year, my pastor and his wife attended a 2014 Global Leader's Summit in Malaysia. Our pastor is part of the International Strategic Alliance of Apostolic Churches (ISAAC) Network led by Dr. Jonathan David, and Dr. David released a very powerful prophetic word during the first session of that annual conference. Fortunately, not only did one of the prophetic voices of our church listen in on this conference while it was streaming live, but she wrote it down and recently shared it in a morning service.

> *Holding Fast to Your Confession and Creating a New World with Your Words* by Jonathan David
>
> God is about to touch your lips afresh so that when you speak you will start to recreate the atmosphere, recreate the environment, and change things. By faith they understood that God spoke things into being. This is going to become your portion. God is going to give you a supernatural grace so that when you open your mouth and begin to speak, your world will start to be redesigned— start to reshape and redesign your world. God is touching your lips and placing His word on your mouth so that at the sound of His word things will start to accelerate, chain reactions will start to take place.
>
> Holy Spirit shows me that He is going to give you the power to articulate, power to speak, power to proclaim, power to declare, to articulate with clarity and wisdom. *When you open your mouth and speak, things* will *begin to happen.* Even as He spoke the word and said, "Let there

be light" and there was light, so will be the Word of God on your mouth. *And when you start to hold fast to the confession of your faith and stay true to what you believe and start to speak, you will start to recreate a whole new world.* Your world is going to change. Stop accepting your world, stop adapting to your world, stop compromising and being conformed to your world. The devil has been speaking and shaping your world. It is time for you to speak back, talk back—declare back. It is time for you to launch a massive attack on the enemy.

Begin to speak what God has spoken to you; what you speak will become the material for the new world. The Lord is saying you are going to redesign your ministry, redesign your life, even redesign your own health, and redesign your family by speaking the word of life given to you. Stop living in and accepting the world that is being thrown at you by the devil ... that is not your world. *Your world is what God has spoken to you.* Your world is going to be a new world, a world subdued under the power of the Holy Ghost. He is going to subject the world to come not to angels but to those who have faith and will speak the word of life. He is going to bring the entire world to subjection to the word of life that He is going to speak.

As soon as I heard this word, I knew that it was a word that should be released to *you,* the reader. I declare that it will bless, encourage, and cause you to walk in all of the things prophesied here; and may you victoriously overcome every situation you face now and going forward. Furthermore, may God's will be done in your life as He has already declared it in the heavenly places. May you powerfully co-labor with God and Christ Jesus through His Holy Spirit and *pull down* all of the resources of heaven, *shut up* the forces of evil, and *advance* God's kingdom in the earth as He has spoken to you in the heavenly places (on earth as it is in heaven)! Amen!

Chapter 11

On Earth as It Is in Heaven

Your kingdom come. *Your will be done on earth as it is in heaven.* (Matt. 6:10)

The Lord has established His throne in heaven, and His kingdom rules over all. (Ps. 103:19)

Blessed *be* the God and Father of our Lord Jesus Christ, who has blessed us with every spiritual blessing in the heavenly places in Christ. (Eph. 1:3)

I will give you the keys of the kingdom of heaven; and whatever you bind (declare to be improper and unlawful) on earth must be what is already bound in heaven; and whatever you loose (declare lawful) on earth must be what is already loosed in heaven. (Matt. 16:19 AMP)

Jesus Taught a New Way of Praying, But Not Like This

When Jesus outlined how He wanted people to pray, He gave some very specific dos and don'ts. He first started with several don'ts, one of which is outlined in Matthew 6:7–8, where Jesus said, "And when you pray, *do not use vain repetitions as the heathen do. For they think that they will be heard for their many words.* Therefore do not be like them. For your Father knows the things you have need of before you ask Him" (emphasis added).

What exactly is a vain repetition? The online *Merriam-Webster* dictionary first defines *vain* as "having no real value; idle or worthless." Second, it defines *vain* as "marked by futility or ineffectualness; unsuccessful or useless." Last, *vain* is also defined as "archaic; foolish or silly." We all know that *repetition* basically means to do the same thing over and over again. Now when you do something over and over again and do not see any results, then clearly this is an example of ultimate foolishness or silliness.

Jesus instructed us not to pray like the heathen because they think that God will hear them because of their many, repetitious, and useless words. Clearly, God is not tuned into this type of prayer; otherwise Jesus would not have told them to instead "pray in this manner," which He described in verses 8–13. So the point that I am making is that *if* we are praying to God in this way, we need to stop now if we want Him to respond to our prayers. Because based on what Jesus said in Matthew 6:7, I can conclude that God does not hear, let alone answer, this type of prayer. I recognize that this concept may be difficult for some people to swallow, particularly if you have been praying this way for a very long time. But I encourage you to ask Holy Spirit to reveal the truth of Jesus's important words about prayer to your heart, spirit, and mind so that you can quickly come into full agreement and proper alignment with the method of prayer that *He* wants us to use when we pray. The good news is that we have the Helper to show us how we should be praying.

So Pray like This

At least Jesus did not leave us hanging or leave us to figure out how to pray on our own. He was very specific about how we should pray to *our Father who is in heaven,* not some foreign god in La-la land. In verses 9 and 10 of Matthew 6, He said, "In this manner, therefore, pray: Our Father in heaven, Hallowed be Your name. Your kingdom come. Your will be done on earth as it is in heaven." We are to look at God as our Father—and a *good* father at that. A good father does right by his child and will care, teach, protect, provide, and do everything in his power to ensure that he raises his child so that he or she has the best chance for success. God is no different. In fact, Jesus said later in Luke 11:11–13, "If a son asks for bread from any father among you, will he give him a stone? Or if he asks for a fish, will he give him a serpent instead of a fish? Or if he asks for an egg, will he offer him a scorpion? If you then, being evil, know how to give good gifts to your children, how much more will your heavenly Father give the Holy Spirit to those who ask Him!"

The key is that we recognize that we serve a good and generous God and He desires to give us good things. So when we pray from the throne room and we are willing to declare those things that God and Christ are praying around the throne, we can then be assured that those are the prayers that will get answered. What is interesting is that these verses from Luke 11:11–13 follow the first part of the Lord's Prayer just seven verses earlier. Jesus outlined the method of how we are to pray and then told them in verse 9, "So I say to you, *ask, and it will be given to you; seek, and you will find; knock, and it will be opened to you*" (emphasis added). Again, Jesus told us how to pray and then gave us permission to ask, seek, and knock. He then assured us of a promise that those things would be fulfilled. What a wonderful God we serve!

We Pray to Our Father in Heaven

Remember—we are not praying to some ethereal and nebulous god somewhere out there, one who lives in a mystery place that only a few seem to know about. Yes, there are plenty of individuals who think we are "slow" or downright idiotic for believing that there is a heaven—even worse that we would pray to some so-called being that they say no one has ever seen. That's okay, because 1 Corinthians 2:14 confirms: "But the natural man does not receive the things of the Spirit of God, for they are foolishness to him; nor can he know them, because they are spiritually discerned." If we walk by the spirit, then we will understand spiritual things; but if we choose not to walk by the spirit, then it is *impossible* to understand or even believe what I am saying. So if the naysayers think you're dumb for believing in all of this, it's totally okay because they really do not have the capacity to understand. At the end of the day, we will all have to give an account to God.

Ephesians 1:3 says, "Blessed be the God and Father of our Lord Jesus Christ, who has blessed us with every spiritual blessing in the heavenly places in Christ" and in verse 5, "having predestined us to adoption as sons by Jesus Christ to Himself, according to the good pleasure of His will." We see here in these amazing Scriptures that the God and Father of Jesus has blessed us with every spiritual blessing in the heavenly places in Christ Jesus and that He has *already* predestined us to adoption as sons. So if Jesus said to pray to our Father in heaven, we are praying as sons— just as He is the Son. This is critical because so much of the body of Christ prays from the position of beggars and servants, not as sons. In addition to the Lord's Prayer, Galatians 4:6–7 justifies our sonship: "And because you are sons, God has sent forth the Spirit of His Son into your hearts, crying out, "Abba, Father!" Therefore you are no longer a slave but a son, and if a son, then an heir of God through Christ."

So from now on, when we come before our Father in heaven, we need to recognize that He is a good father, one who has already blessed us with every spiritual blessing in the heavenly places in Christ Jesus. Not only that, but we are sons, not servants or beggars, and we get to come before our Father in the throne room. Additionally, when we operate from the throne room, we are then privy to what the Father is doing because Jesus through His spirit makes those things known to us. John 15:15 says, "No longer do I call you slaves, for the slave does not know what his master is doing; but I have called you friends, for all things that I have heard from my Father I have made known to you." I don't know about you, but this revelation and powerful truth is so exciting to me because we get to partner in on what God, our Father in heaven, is saying and doing and then release His will into the earth.

Your Kingdom Come

If there is a king, then there must be a kingdom. Jesus is the King of Kings and the Lord of Lords, so He definitely has a kingdom. Mark 16:19

says, "So then, after the Lord had spoken to them, He was received up into heaven, and sat down at the right hand of God." Psalm 103:19 says, "The Lord has established His throne in heaven, and His kingdom rules over all." So now that we can easily see that there is a king who has a kingdom and that His kingdom is in the heavenly places, let's go back and see what Jesus said in Matthew 6:10: "Your kingdom come …" I'd like to let the Word of God define some of the most important truths regarding His kingdom.

Twelve Kingdom Truths

1. For the kingdom of God is not eating and drinking, but righteousness and peace and joy in the Holy Spirit. (Rom. 14:17)
2. For the kingdom of God is not in word but in power. (1 Cor. 4:20)
3. But He said to them, "I must preach the kingdom of God to the other cities also, because for this purpose I have been sent." (Luke 4:43)
4. … and saying, "The time is fulfilled, and the kingdom of God is at hand. Repent, and believe in the gospel." (Mark 1:15)
5. Jesus answered and said to him, "Most assuredly, I say to you, unless one is born again, he cannot see the kingdom of God." (John 3:3)
6. Jesus answered, "Most assuredly, I say to you, unless one is born of water and the Spirit, he cannot enter the kingdom of God." (John 3:5)
7. Assuredly, I say to you, whoever does not receive the kingdom of God as a little child will by no means enter it. (Mark 10:15)
8. But seek first the kingdom of God and His righteousness, and all these things shall be added to you. (Matt. 6:33)
9. And I bestow upon you a kingdom, just as My Father bestowed one upon Me. (Luke 22:29)
10. And He said, "To you it has been given to know the mysteries of the kingdom of God, but to the rest it is given in parables, that 'Seeing they may not see, And hearing they may not understand.'" (Luke 8:10)

11. And *I* will give you the keys of the kingdom of heaven, and whatever you bind on earth will be bound in heaven, and whatever you loose on earth will be loosed in heaven." (Matt. 16:19)
12. And as you go, preach, saying, "The kingdom of heaven is at hand." (Matt. 10:7)

We can see some very powerful truths about the kingdom of God in these Scriptures. First, the kingdom of God is righteousness, peace, and joy in the Holy Spirit, and His kingdom is not in word but in *power*. Jesus was sent for the purpose of preaching God's kingdom. He also said that the time was fulfilled and the kingdom of God was at hand, meaning that God's kingdom is near us. Jesus represented the kingdom of God and when He came to earth, God's kingdom was brought near. When we accept Jesus as our personal Lord and Savior, then He lives in us and we live in Him, and therefore *the kingdom of God is in us* and goes wherever we go! Just like Jesus changed the atmosphere of every place that He went, we likewise get to change the atmosphere of every place that we go. Why? Because the kingdom of God is at hand!

This is a powerful concept when we understand that the kingdom of God is within us. Luke 17:21 verifies this: "Nor will they say, 'See here!' or 'See there!' *For indeed, the kingdom of God is within you*" (emphasis added). *We* are the kingdom of God manifested here on earth, and it's when God works in and through us that we and others get to see His kingdom in action. When we are born again and born of water and of the spirit, then we get to not only *see* but *enter* into God's kingdom. We must receive the kingdom of God as a little child who simply trusts and does not try to rationalize everything.

Our pastor gave a powerful illustration of what it means to receive the kingdom of God with childlike faith. He told a story about his grandchildren coming over for the weekend. He had recently bought a house that sits on many acres, and a river flows through the back of the property. The area surrounding the river had grown over, and although he could hear the river, he couldn't see it. So over a few weeks, the area had been cleared so the river could be seen. When the kids came over, they brought their rubber boots because they were excitedly *expecting* to go down to the river.

Our pastor strictly warned the kids not to go near the water, but before he knew it, they were standing in it. He chastised them and told them not to go any farther. He said he turned around for a minute and when he turned back around, they were standing in knee deep, excitedly yelling that the water was running into their boots! He couldn't believe how bold and fearless these kids were and how they kept pushing the boundary.

The next thing he knew, the kids were in the water up to their faces. All he could think about was how cold the water must have been given that it was still early spring. He said that he was content with just being able to see the river, but not these kids; they wanted to *enter in* and personally experience the river.

One kid said to the other, "I baptize you in the name of the Father, the Son, and the Holy Spirit!" Our pastor said his jaw hit the ground when he heard this. He realized that as he's gotten older, he'd set up all kinds of limitations on certain things, which he recognized has somewhat prevented him from entering into the *fullness* that God intended. He said that the Lord then challenged him to have that childlike faith and expectancy that He called us to operate in and stop putting so many limitations on Him.

The moral of this story is that we have to allow Holy Spirit to help us remove the limitations, preconceived notions, fears, bad experiences, and everything else that prevents us from being able to fully enter into God's kingdom. These barriers are what keep nations of believers from entering in and experiencing all of the spiritual blessings that God has for us in the heavenly places in Christ Jesus. When we operate with a childlike faith, we can simply trust in the promises outlined in God's Word and thus easily enter into His kingdom. I'm hoping that the example of our pastor's grandkids helps better put into perspective the necessity and importance of having childlike faith when it comes to being able to enter His kingdom.

Not only did God give us a kingdom, but He gave it to us so that we could know its mysteries. Mysteries are things that are hidden or not known, but Jesus said that we will know the mysteries of the kingdom. How will we come into the knowledge of these mysteries? It is only through Holy Spirit and operating from the heavenly places that we will know the mysteries of heaven. While all of this might sound "mysterious," we should not make it complicated. We must trust and believe that we will in fact know the mysteries of the kingdom, just like Jesus said. In the Amplified Bible, Jesus also said that He will give us the keys of the kingdom and whatever we bind on earth must be *what is already bound in heaven* and whatever we loose on earth must be *what is already loosed in heaven.* I look at it this way—if we are operating from the heavenly places and are declaring God's Word into the earth, then whatever we bind in heaven has no choice but to be bound on earth and whatever we loose in heaven has no choice but to be loosed on earth.

For example, if we are led to declare from heaven that a spirit of infirmity or fear be *bound* in our bodies here on earth, then that spirit will have no choice but to leave. Why? Because God's will was already declared; therefore, those spirits must come in line with the word that was spoken in heaven—"on earth as it is in heaven." If we *loose* God's wisdom, favor, grace, mercy, and provision over a specific circumstance, then we should likewise see a manifestation of what we declared in that circumstance. This is exactly what the kingdom of God looks like, and this is the first part of the Lord's Prayer in action. The kingdom is not somewhere far off in the future, but it is here and now; and when we see the manifested power of God working in and through us, then we are participating in God's kingdom.

On Earth as It Is in Heaven

To me, this is one of the most exciting parts of the Lord's Prayer. When Jesus said, "Your kingdom come. Your will be done on earth as it is in heaven," something very powerful was released right there. We have already established what God's kingdom looks like, but this next part tells us *how* it should look. Jesus basically said, "God's kingdom come and His will be done." Where is His will to be done? Here, on earth. How should His will be done? *Exactly as it is in heaven!* When God said, "Let there be light," He spoke that word *from the heavenly places*, and what He spoke there manifested *on earth* exactly as it was declared. In fact, light is *still* continuing to break forth into the universe today.

That one command from heaven back at the beginning of time is still bearing fruit.

It works the same with us. If we hear His Holy Spirit tell us or impress upon us to declare something in the heavenly places, then we should be able to see it manifest on earth exactly as it was declared in heaven. Clearly, we may not immediately see some things that we declare from heaven manifest; however, if it's *truly God's will* that we declare, then we should have the full expectation that we will eventually see it. Remember—God's timing and our timing are not the same. However, that does not mean that we don't walk our declaration out in faith and believe that what He had us declare in heaven will absolutely come to pass on earth, regardless of how long it takes.

All of the Resources of Heaven

Since our spiritual base of operation is from the heavenly places, then all of the resources of heaven are ours as well. This is validated in Ephesians 1:3 when Paul said, "We have been blessed with every spiritual blessing in the heavenly places in Christ." This is significant because so many believers live in great lack, which leads me to conclude that they must not realize that they have *already* been blessed with every single resource they will ever need. One of the missing keys here is that if a believer does not realize that he or she needs to operate from the heavenly places to access these blessings or resources, then it totally makes sense why there is lack.

I once heard someone say that when God gives an assignment, He also provides us with all of the resources necessary to complete it. Those resources are not just physical, but they also include knowledge, wisdom, understanding, discernment, grace, mercy, favor, and so on. All of these things originate from the place of the Spirit, and God's Spirit resides in the heavenly places. God's Holy Spirit also resides in us, and He is our connection to the Father and Christ Jesus. So it is when we operate through Holy Spirit that we are able to easily connect to the heavenly places and *hear* what is going on around the throne of God. This is how we get to operate in the earthly-natural and spiritual-supernatural realms at the same time;

and when we operate from the spiritual-supernatural dimension when we pray, we then get to bring His kingdom and His will on this earth, and it should look exactly like it looks in heaven. This is powerful!

My prayer and declaration is that Holy Spirit would help you grasp the significance and power of the Lord's Prayer. May you be able to engage in this powerful prayer in a fresh, new way, and may you know the will of God when you pray. I declare that when you pray in this manner, all of the strongholds and barriers that have kept you from experiencing breakthrough in the past fall to the ground in the name of Jesus! I declare that as you engage Holy Spirit and enter into this Prayer Pattern, He will give you fresh revelation about those things deep in your heart; and what He gives you to declare may you boldly declare it. May what you declare on earth manifest *exactly* as you declared it in heaven. Let His will be done in your life in the mighty name of Jesus! Amen.

Chapter 12

Keep Your Eyes Fixed on God, Not the Circumstances

For momentary, light affliction is producing for us an eternal weight of glory far beyond all comparison, while we look not at the things which are seen, but at the things which are not seen; for the things which are seen are temporal, but the things which are not seen are eternal. (2 Cor. 4:17–18)

If then you were raised with Christ, seek those things which are above, where Christ is, sitting at the right hand of God. Set your mind on things above, not on things on the earth. (Col. 3:1–2)

My brethren, count it all joy when you fall into various trials, knowing that the testing of your faith produces patience. (James 1:2–3)

There's More to Circumstances Than We May Think

Despite what some believers may think, negative circumstances do not occur to cause us to lose hope or bring destruction upon us. In the Bible, 2 Corinthians 4:17-18 says, "For momentary, light affliction is producing for us an eternal weight of glory ..., but the things which are not seen are eternal." The truth is that our circumstances are momentary and may cause light affliction, but they produce something valuable and far beyond all comparison. This verse also says that we are to not look at or focus on things that are seen but at the things unseen. Why does it say this? It's because the things that can be seen are temporal (not lasting), and the things that cannot be seen are eternal (this life and beyond)—and eternity is where we ultimately want to focus our gaze.

What's the point, here? When we encounter difficult situations, we need to keep our eyes focused on Christ (the unseen and the eternal) and His promises to us, instead of focusing on the circumstance itself (the seen and the temporary). Circumstances in and of themselves are conditional and subject to interpretation. How we view, perceive, and internalize the circumstances that we see assigns meanings, feelings, attitudes, beliefs, and ultimately our actions in that situation. For example, if it rains, one person may say, "Thank God, it's raining," but another person may say, "It's raining. What a horrible day." How can it be that two people view the same exact circumstance so differently? It's because it is not what we see that causes the feelings, either positive or negative, but it's *how we view or perceive what we see* that brings about a particular set of thoughts, feelings, and subsequent actions.

We can look to the story of David and Goliath to see an incredibly relevant and powerful example of what keeping things in their proper perspective looks like in practical terms. Here's the scenario. Saul and the men of Israel were gathered together and encamped on one side of the mountain in the Valley of Elah; and Goliath and the Philistines were on the other side of that same mountain. Goliath, who was their fiercest warrior and also happened to be over nine feet tall, shouted taunts at the Israelites for forty days and nights. The Israelites heard all of his insolent taunts, and as a result, they all fled and were locked down in fear.

Young David's father sent him with food to feed his brothers, and when David got there, he wanted to know why everyone was so fearful. His brothers told him about Goliath and his threats, but unlike them, he had no fear. In fact, he made a bold statement: "What shall be done for the man who kills this Philistine and takes away the reproach from

Israel? For who is this uncircumcised Philistine, that he should defy the armies of the living God?" (1 Sam. 17:26). Verse 32 adds, "Then David said to Saul, 'Let no man's heart fail because of him; your servant will go and fight with this Philistine.'" Saul expressed his doubt about David in verse 33, saying, "You are not able to go against this Philistine to fight with him; for you are a youth, and he a man of war from his youth."

David told Saul in verses 34–35 about his experiences as a shepherd: "Your servant used to keep his father's sheep, and when a lion or a bear came and took a lamb out of the flock, I went out after it and struck it, and delivered the lamb from its mouth; and when it arose against me, I caught it by its beard, and struck and killed it." Then David makes a bold claim in verse 36: "Your servant has killed both lion and bear; and this uncircumcised Philistine will be like one of them, seeing he has defied the armies of the living God." Moreover David said, "The Lord, who delivered me from the paw of the lion and from the paw of the bear, He will deliver me from the hand of this Philistine."

Are you starting to get the picture here? None of Goliath's taunts had any impact on David! David was as bold as a lion. Furthermore, Goliath was nearly twice as tall as David and armed to the hilt, but this did not faze David. Why? Because David had his eyes squarely fixed on God and how big *He* was, not on some loudmouth giant shouting blasphemous threats. The Israelites, on the other hand, were completely transfixed by the size and sound of Goliath and his threats and had completely lost sight of the God who had protected and blessed Israel for generations. In David's eyes, Goliath was already under his feet because he knew that the Lord was the one who would deliver him from Goliath's hand. This is precisely why David could display the confidence and boldness that we read about in this account.

So what happened? When David approached Goliath to fight him, Goliath was indignant that such a young boy would dare come out to fight him. Verses 43–44 say, "The Philistine said to David, 'Am I a dog that you come to me with sticks?' And the Philistine cursed David by his gods. And the Philistine said to David, 'Come to me, and I will give your flesh to the birds of the air and the beasts of the field!'" The beautiful thing is that David was not even remotely moved by this threat. In fact, he said in verses 45–47, "You come to me with a sword, with a spear, and with a javelin. But I come to you in the name of the Lord of hosts, the God of the armies of Israel, whom you have defied. This day the Lord will deliver you into my hand, and I will strike you and take your head from you. And this day I will give the carcasses of the camp of the Philistines to the birds of the air and the wild beasts of the earth, that all the earth may know that there is a God in Israel. Then all this assembly shall know that the Lord does not save with sword and spear; for the battle is the Lord's, and He will give you into our hands." That's what I'm talking about—true boldness and confidence in the Lord of hosts!

Most of us know the dreadful outcome for Goliath. David killed him with a single shot and cut his head off with Goliath's own sword. When the Philistines saw that their champion was dead, they fled. Ha! Who was on the run now? This story is so awesome because this is how *we* need to look at every single circumstance that comes our way. There should be *nothing* that causes us to shrink back and hide. We should be able to exhibit the same and even more confidence than David because Christ secured the victory for us over two thousand years ago. As a result, we get to go into every trial knowing that we have the victory and that the Enemy is under our feet! The situation with David and Goliath is a perfect example of what it looks like to keep your eyes squarely fixed on God and not be moved by the circumstance, no matter how big or impressive it is in the natural.

You Get to Choose

One thing that I have learned over the last many years is that I am the one who gets to choose how I will respond to a given situation or circumstance. I have heard so many people say things like, "Oh, the Devil is really working me over," "I wish the Enemy would get off my back," "If it were not for bad luck, I would not have any luck at all," "God is causing so many bad things to happen to me," and countless other interesting phrases that describe how they perceive their circumstances. *We* are the ones who control how we view what we see and how we will respond. News flash—the Devil has *no power* to make you think, perceive, believe, or react to what comes your way. There is no human on this earth who possesses that power either. God gave us free will, and we get to *choose* how we will respond to the things that come before us.

Thus far, most of the chapters in this book highlight the truth of who you are in Christ, that you have an inheritance, that you have Holy Spirit as your guide, and that you get to operate in two dimensions at the same time—here on earth and your spiritual base in the heavenly places. But I'd like to remind you right now that we are the ones who have authority over our circumstances, and we should realize that those circumstances are there for the purposes of making us more Christlike, building our character, and bringing us closer to Christ, not for destroying us or making us miserable.

I encourage you to take those things you perceive as negative or that you don't understand straight to the Lord and ask Him how you should respond and where He wants you to go from there. I promise that when you go to God about the issue, allow Holy Spirit to guide you through the process, and follow (obey) His instructions, you will successfully get through *everything* that comes before you. This is not to say that the situation will always go your way, but you will have peace in the storm, and God will work all of those things out for your good and not your harm, because that's how He operates. The following Scriptures should give you sufficient courage to at least try this approach if you have not done so before or do it more often if it is not a regular practice. Remember—the victory is yours!

> For I know the thoughts that I think toward you, says the Lord, thoughts of peace and not of evil, to give you a future and a hope. Then you will call upon Me and go and pray to Me, and I will listen to you. And you will seek Me and find Me, when you search for Me with all your heart. I will be found by you, says the Lord, and I will bring you back from your captivity; I will gather you from all the nations and from all the places where I have driven you, says the Lord, and I will bring you

to the place from which I cause you to be carried away captive. (Jer. 29:11–14)

And we know that all things work together for good to those who love God, to those who are the called according to His purpose. (Rom. 8:28)

Count It All Joy!

When I first read the Scripture from James 1 many years ago, I wondered if James was on something when he said that we should count it all joy when we fall into various trials. I don't know about you, but when I used to think about trials and tribulations, *joy* would definitely not be in my top one thousand words that I would ever think of to describe the disposition that I should have when trials and tribulations come my way.

That old mind-set changed when I began to learn that God was the one who allowed me to go through various trials for the express purpose of bringing about specific outcomes; only then could I even see that He was trying to establish my character and integrity, as well as shape and form me into the image of Christ. I was beginning to see and, more importantly, understand the beneficial aspects of going through trials and tribulations, otherwise known as our circumstances.

I also uncovered through the trials that I faced that God wanted me to establish a much deeper level of intimacy with Him, Christ Jesus, and Holy Spirit. Through that intimacy, I then started learning *how* to navigate through the trials by keeping my eyes squarely fixed on Jesus and not on the circumstances. He taught me that when I keep my eyes fixed on Him in the heavenly place, then all the other things—the circumstances—will come into proper perspective. Holy Spirit also showed me that whatever holds my focus will become magnified, so if my eyes are fixed on Christ, then all I can see are His promises, His love for me, and His power to help me overcome anything before me. Conversely, if I focus more on the problem, then *it* will become magnified, and all I will be able to see is fear, despair, discouragement, hopelessness, and anything else that can come when the problem becomes magnified.

Remember that, two years ago, Robert and my younger sister were looking at the situation with my other sister, and all they could see was size of the situation and how bad it looked. Their lenses of fear brought about more fear, and that fear could only see negative outcomes. On the other hand, my mom and I fixed our gaze on God, which allowed us to see things the way that He saw them. As a result of keeping our eyes fixed on Jesus, we were able access the strategies of heaven, declare forth what He had to say about it, and eventually see her break free from her captivity—*once and for all!*

As I learned how to view my circumstances from my position of being seated with Christ and in Christ, I was better able to successfully navigate through every trial that came before me. I'd even go so far as to say that in most of those trials, there was an expediency that I had never encountered before. It was almost as if, once I focused on what God was saying about that particular circumstance instead of the circumstance *itself*, He was able to show me exactly what was going on, how I should be responding, and then lead me through to safe passage. I must note that some trials took longer to navigate simply because God was working on things according to His timing. The good news is that I had the peace and grace I needed to endure those circumstances until He brought them to completion.

We can also look at Psalm 23:4 to see a beautiful illustration of this truth: "Yea, though I walk through the valley of the shadow of death, I will fear no evil; for You are with me; Your rod and Your staff, they comfort me." The truth is that God, through His Holy Spirit, leads us through the circumstances; we don't just lie down and stay there for the rest of our lives, and we don't die there either. I found that there is an abundance of wisdom, knowledge, discernment, and understanding available for everything I face. Holy Spirit showed me that God is much bigger than *any* circumstance and that Christ in me already gave me the victory over two thousand years ago. All I need to do is enforce that victory in every circumstance—no matter how big and impressive it may appear in the natural.

God taught me the importance of *immediately* bringing all circumstances before Him and that I should not be asking *why* something is happening to me, but instead, I am to ask *how* I should respond and what He wants to show me. When I learned to respond in that way, *everything* in my life changed. After all, I wanted to know His will and purpose for each circumstance and situation, which is exactly what Jesus meant when He said, "Your kingdom come, *your will be done, on earth as it is in heaven*" (emphasis added). Jesus gave us the model of how we are to pray because He knew that God's will is always the right thing to pray. After inquiring about how I should respond to the various circumstances in my life, Holy Spirit would always give me what to declare over those situations, thus, declaring that God's will be done. He also gave me the strategies and tactics that I should employ for the battles ahead. It's one thing to declare over the circumstances, but we also need to know *what* to do and *how* to do when in these difficult places.

God Can Be Trusted in Your Trials

The biggest thing that God showed me in all of this was that I can trust Him with those things that He allows me to encounter. He also showed me that I already have the victory when facing any situation and that He would never let me fall or hang out there with no guidance or protection. When I completely trust God, there is always an abundance of His peace and joy, even when the circumstance is the literal death of someone I deeply love. God showed me that when I look to Him for the wisdom to handle every situation, even something as small as how I should respond to a questionable email, then His perfect solution is always provided.

Over the years, trusting God became the norm, and navigating trials has become a lot more productive and rewarding and, yes, joyful—joyful because I am always assured that the victory is mine and that I get to co-labor with God and Christ through every circumstance. Although it took many, many years to learn how to develop a Christlike response to various circumstances, I have become a completely new and transformed person in the process. My vision in every circumstance has tremendously expanded, and my outlook for the future is exceedingly bright. I now know that every trial that God allows to come before me is expressly for the purpose of growing closer to Him, accomplishing His will in the earth, removing character flaws, becoming more Christlike, preparing me for the next assignment, and giving Him the glory that He so richly deserves. I'd also like to point out that it was the lessons I learned from Holy Spirit in difficult trials that caused me to grow the most. Difficult? Yes. Worth it? Absolutely!

The truth in all of this is that in every trial, circumstance, or situation we face, it is imperative that we *immediately* look to God, Christ Jesus, and Holy Spirit for how we should respond. I love that God gave us free will when He created us and that we always have the choice of what we will focus on when we face circumstances. We can choose to be in fear by doubting, worrying, and believing the lies of the Enemy, or we can choose to trust God by believing the promises in His Word and that His plans for our good far outweigh any plans the Enemy has for our harm.

Remember—whatever we choose to focus on will always become magnified. If we focus on God instead of the circumstance, then He will become far bigger in that situation; consequently, the circumstance will become much smaller and will not appear as big and scary as we might have initially thought. If we know that we have a godly solution to our circumstances and the power and authority to back it up, then we will have much more confidence when facing those difficult trials. But it's guaranteed that if we focus on the problem, then that thing will appear much bigger than it actually is. As a result, God will be significantly diminished in our eyes, and if we're not careful, we could lose sight of Him altogether. Basically, we need to start telling our circumstances how big our God is rather than tell God how big our circumstance is. Trust me, He is not fazed or overwhelmed by *anything* you bring before Him! Lost car keys or end-stage cancer- it matters not to God.

I'm declaring that you'll grab hold of what I have shared and that there will be acceleration for you as you maneuver through your own circumstances and trials. I believe that what took me years to learn will take months and what took me months will only take weeks or days for you to learn.

I declare that Holy Spirit would quickly illuminate your eyes so that you can see what's actually going on in your circumstances and that you will not be fooled by the fear that the Enemy projects at you. May you experience the peace and joy of Christ as you navigate through every circumstance that comes your way. I declare that you will develop a deeper confidence that allows you to boldly move forward and obtain the victory that you have already been promised through Christ Jesus!

I declare that the eyes and ears of your understanding will be enlightened so that you will step exactly how God wants you to step. May you come into a richer knowledge of the faith that you possess and come to believe that He has amazing plans and purposes for your life, and that through Christ, you are able to accomplish everything that He sets before you. Amen.

Chapter 13

Don't Buy the Lie—The Devil Ain't All That!

Having disarmed principalities and powers, He made a public spectacle of them, triumphing over them in it. (Col. 2:15)

Inasmuch then as the children have partaken of flesh and blood, He Himself likewise shared in the same, that through death He might destroy him who had the power of death, that is, the devil, and release those who through fear of death were all their lifetime subject to bondage. (Heb. 2:14–15)

Above all, taking the shield of faith with which you will be able to quench all the fiery darts of the wicked one. (Eph. 6:16)

Have I not commanded you? Be strong and of good courage; *do not be afraid*, nor be dismayed, for the Lord your God is with you wherever you go. (Joshua 1:9)

Oh, No—Not that Spooky Devil Talk Again!

When it comes to talking about the Devil and dark spiritual forces, I don't know what happens to some Christians, but they get all weirded out. I've even heard some believers refuse to talk about the subject because they say it's "too spooky and scary." Seriously? I guess I can understand where some of these fears come from, especially with what Hollywood has done to heighten the fear factor associated with the topic, but I am here to remind of you of some very important truths that will help to put things in better perspective. The main truth in all of this is that "through Christ's death, he might destroy him who had the power of death, that is, the devil" (Heb. 2:14). We must never forget that Christ defeated the power of the Devil and allowed us to be conveyed or transferred into His kingdom; therefore, we should have nothing to fear when it comes to the things of darkness. Remember, we are seated with Christ and in Christ in the heavenly places, and those places are far above all principalities and powers. Therefore, the Enemy is already under our feet and we have authority over him!

Truth Number 1: God's got your back!

> Have I not commanded you? Be strong and of good courage; do not be afraid, nor be dismayed, for the Lord your God is with you wherever you go. (Joshua 1:9)

> > But the Lord is faithful, who will establish you and guard you from the evil one. (2 Thess. 3:3)

We can very clearly see from these two Scriptures that not only is God with us wherever we go, but He promises to guard us from the evil one. We must *believe* these truths if we are going to be successful against the attacks of the Enemy. We know from 1 Peter 5:8 that we should "Be sober, be vigilant; because your adversary the devil walks about like a roaring lion, seeking whom he may devour." The question here is not about *if* the Devil will launch assaults against believers; it's about *when* those attacks will come. If we do not believe that God has our backs and will protect us from the evil one or that greater is He

(Christ) who is in us than he (the devil) who is in the world, then it's going to be incredibly difficult to live the life of victory that Christ intended.

When we fear what we think the Devil can do to us *more* than we trust God to protect us, then we are in essence saying that Satan has greater power than God. While this might sound harsh, think about it—why then do some Christians allow the Enemy to kick their rear ends all over God's green earth and defeat them on most every level of life? It's because they have not encountered the truth of who they are in Christ Jesus and recognized that they are "seated with and in Christ in the heavenly places, far above all principality and power and might and dominion, and every name that is named, not only in this age but also in that which is to come" (Eph. 1:21). By spiritually operating from the heavenly places, we are afforded a supernatural protection that cannot be penetrated by the Enemy.

Conversely, believers who walk in the knowledge of this great truth have absolutely no fear of the Devil and his works because we know where the *real* power lies, and it is *not* with Satan! We also realize that because Christ is in us and we operate with His power and authority, then we get to operate with a high degree of boldness and courage. If God told Joshua to be strong and of good courage and not to be afraid, nor be dismayed, then how much bolder and of greater courage should we walk in with The Lion of the Tribe of Judah resident on the inside of us? The bottom line is that believers should *never* walk in fear of the Enemy—*ever!*

Truth Number 2: Seriously, the Devil ain't all that.

> How you are fallen from heaven, *O Lucifer,* son of the morning! *How you are cut down to the ground,* You who weakened the nations! *For you have said in your heart: "I will ascend into heaven, I will exalt my throne above the stars of God;* I will also sit on the mount of the congregation on the farthest sides of the north."... *Yet you shall be brought down to Sheol, to the lowest depths of the Pit. Those who see you will gaze at you, and consider you,* saying:

> "*Is this the man who made the earth tremble*, who shook kingdoms, who made the world as a wilderness and destroyed its cities, who did not open the house of his prisoners?" (Is. 14:12–13, 15–17, emphasis added)

> And He said to them, "I saw Satan fall like lightning from heaven." (Luke 10:18)

> So the great dragon was cast out, that serpent of old, called the Devil and Satan, who deceives the whole world; he was cast to the earth, and his angels were cast out with him. (Rev. 12:9)

The depiction here is that Satan, who was formerly known as the angel Lucifer, was cast to the earth and also brought down to the lowest depths of "the Pit." I particularly like the reference in Isaiah 14:16, where those who saw him in the pit gazed at him in wonder and asked if this could really be the one who did all the damage described in verses 16 and 17. It was almost like they were in awe that someone that they thought and truly believed had such great power was nothing more than a fallen fool at the bottom of a pit. This ought to be the same picture that we have of Satan today—a being that has had his authority over believers completely stripped away by Christ's resurrection and that is incapable of bringing weapons that can prosper against us.

This kind of reminds me of the power that the Wizard of Oz seemed to have over the land and people of Oz. Everyone, especially Dorothy, thought that this ruler was the only one with the ability to solve their problems. It wasn't until they went behind the curtain that they realized that he was just an ordinary man who used a lot smoke and mirrors to deceive everyone and make people think that he was far bigger than he actually was. Satan works in the same exact way. He uses a lot of smoke and mirrors to create the perception that he is bigger than he actually is.

Let's take another look at the Scripture from 1 Peter 5:8: "that we should be sober, be vigilant; because your adversary the devil walks about like a roaring lion, seeking whom he may devour." First, the Word says that we need to be vigilant when it comes to the Devil. *Merriam-Webster* defines *vigilant* as "alertly watchful especially to avoid danger," so this means that we need to be especially watchful when it comes to the schemes of the Enemy. The next part of this verse is perhaps even more critical because it tells us that our adversary, the Devil, walks about *like* a roaring lion. Notice that it does not say that he *is* a roaring lion; it says that he is perpetrating *as though* he is a lion. But let's be clear—he is *not* a lion!

I heard a joke that asked, How does a serpent in the book of Genesis become a dragon by the book of Revelation? Because someone has been feeding him. By believing the lies that the Devil perpetrates, he becomes more powerful in people's lives. It's my observation that many Christians buy into the loudness and aggressive nature of the roar and then falsely conclude that there must be a lion close by that can do them serious bodily harm. This is a lie. Let me remind you of the truth in this powerful scripture. The Devil is *seeking* someone whom he *may* devour. Again, this is critical because it says that he is looking for opportunities to tear someone from limb to limb—not that he *will* devour us. The point here is to get you to realize that the Devil uses lots of trickery to deceive people, and he's looking for those of whom he can take advantage. Remember—it's nearly impossible to be deceived when you intimately know the Truth, who is Jesus!

We are expressly told in Ephesians 4:27, "And do not give the devil an opportunity." That means that we do not want to put ourselves in situations where the Enemy has an advantage and can easily take us out. Let's look at the natural example of the animal kingdom to illustrate this spiritual situation: Which animals do lions usually target? Lions usually hunt weak or sick animals and those that, for whatever reason, have become isolated from the rest of the pack. Likewise, we become targets for an enemy attack when we try to walk *in our own strength* versus walking in the strength of the Lord, have hardened or spiritually sick hearts, or think that we can be lone rangers in our Christian walks. Again, let's not give the Enemy reasons or occasions to attack us; let's instead walk in our full identity of Christ where we have the promises of being more than conquerors.

Truth Number 3: Resist the Devil, and he will flee.

> Therefore submit to God. Resist the devil and he will
> flee from you. (James 4:7)

There are two vital keys that we can take away from this important Scripture. The first is that when the Devil comes looking for trouble, which he usually does, then we are to immediately submit to God. When we are vigilant and watchful, then God through His Holy Spirit will alert us to the Enemy's attacks. It's at that moment that we need to stop in our tracks and submit to *however* Holy Spirit leads us in a given situation. Submission and obedience are two ways that we can stop the Enemy in his tracks.

Second, we need to resist whatever it is that the Enemy is throwing our way. I've learned how to do this through many, many tests and trials; and only when I was able to obey *how* Holy Spirit was leading me at the time could I see the way to break free from the attacks of the Enemy. I remember one instance in particular when my husband and I were in a bit of a spat, and he said something to me that I did not like one bit. I so desperately wanted to lob a choice and juicy verbal bomb his way, but Holy Spirit told me to be quiet and to not say what I was about to say. The *temptation* to throw that bomb was so strong that I had to physically bite down on my finger to keep from launching it. I swear that I was close to drawing blood because I so badly wanted to hurl a nasty insult at my husband—sad but true.

However, when I submitted to the directive of Holy Spirit and kept my big mouth shut, that incredibly strong temptation to throw the verbal missile my husband's way completely passed. What I realized was that the Devil fled because I did not give him an opportunity by saying the mean and nasty thing that I so badly wanted to say. What Holy Spirit showed me in the spirit was that a huge hurricane was coming my way and it was slated to bring great damage, but when I chose the route of silence, it redirected the storm and it went in the opposite direction. Within about thirty minutes or so, the thing that my husband had been fussing about was no longer important, and we were able to move on with no further incident. Scripture backs this up. Proverbs 15:1 says that A gentle answer turns away wrath,

But a harsh word stirs up anger. In my case, a gentle answer was silence, and this silence had the power to turn away the impending anger and wrath that usually follows. The strategies of God are amazing and are totally superior to any of the tactics the enemy might tempt you with.

The point in telling you this is so that you can first recognize the tactics of the Enemy and perhaps choose a different response than you would have in times past. If you make the decision to try *Prayer Pattern* and go after the negative circumstances in your life, then I want you to be aware that this decision will not go uncontested. But if you are vigilant and are not ignorant of the Enemy's devices, then you will be able to *boldly stand* against those attacks, and you will subsequently watch him flee time after time. Remember—the Devil roams around *like* a roaring lion looking for whom he *may* devour. I'm declaring that "the whom" he is looking for *will not be you* but that through Holy Spirit you will see him coming, immediately submit to God, strongly resist his every attack, and watch his Ugliness flee in the name of Jesus!

Truth Number 4: Faith is the ticket.

> Above all, taking the shield of faith with which you will be able to quench all the fiery darts of the wicked one. (Eph. 6:16)

> "No weapon that is formed against you will prosper; and every tongue that accuses you in judgment you will condemn. This is the heritage of the servants of the Lord, and their vindication is from Me," declares the Lord. (Is. 54:17)

The importance of faith referenced in Ephesians 6:16 is significant. Our faith in God, not faith in our own faith, faith in anything or anyone else, causes us to be able to defend against the Enemy's *every* attack. We see that this shield of faith is sufficient to thwart every single thing the wicked one throws our way. I don't know about you, but when I read this and realize the significance of our faith in God, I get pretty excited. What this Scripture is saying is that there is nothing, or "no thing," the Enemy can throw at us that our faith in God can't quench! God's Word promises that no weapon formed against us will prosper, which includes everything the Enemy forms against us.

Here's the deal. I'd go so far as to say that the size, and therefore the effectiveness, of our faith shield is directly proportioned to the size of our faith in God. The bigger our faith and trust in God is, the bigger our shield to block the Enemy's attacks will be. Some years ago, God gave me a picture of what weak faith looks like. He showed me that when our faith in Him is weak, it is the equivalent to our holding up a blanket as our shield instead of a heavy metal shield. This imagery represents spiritual immaturity and its implications.

Think about that for a minute. If you are holding up a blanket to block out the fiery darts being thrown at you by the Enemy, that blanket is not going to be sturdy enough to be effective. Not only that, but if there is some wind blowing, then before you know it, that thing will be flapping around, hitting you in the face, and obstructing your view. Furthermore, these weak faith blankets are not even fire retardant and therefore can easily catch fire when those fiery darts are hurled your way. While this imagery might draw a chuckle, it illustrates the danger of having weak faith in God.

When there is little or weak faith in God, we might be able to block out *some* of the Enemy's fiery arrows, but the point is that the effectiveness of our shield, which in this case is analogous to a blanket, is very limited. The shield of faith referenced in verse 16 says that we can quench or extinguish *all* those fiery darts that are lobbed our way—not some, but all. That's what I'm talking about—*all!*

Now that we understand the relationship between our faith in God and our ability to effectively defend against the attacks of the Enemy, I'd like to focus on the fiery darts of the wicked one. How do those fiery darts most commonly impact us? Fiery darts can come in many forms.

- Guilt
- Condemnation

- Depression
- Intimidation
- Worry and doubt
- Shame
- Accusation
- Oppression
- Temptation
- Questioning your identity
- Fear and anxiety
- Fear of lack or loss
- Telling you that you can't do what God already told you to do
- Getting you to think that flesh and blood (other humans) are the real enemy
- Telling you that you can't possibly hear God
- Using negative circumstances to get you to take your eyes off of God
- Getting you to believe that your situation will never change

The point here is that when the wicked one shoots his best and choicest arrows our way, then *all* of those fiery darts should be extinguished by our shield of faith in God *before* they get to us and do any damage. I've heard it said that it is always easier to keep the enemy out than it is to get him out. After all, it will be much more difficult for the believer to gain ground in the kingdom of God if the enemy already has ground in the believer.

We must remember that when we see the Enemy's arrows coming (the *temptation* to accept one of his many lies), we need to immediately submit to God (by seeking Him and His Word and applying that truth to our given situation) and resist the Devil by believing, trusting, and obeying God's Word rather than the lie. The Word promises that the Devil *will flee* when we do—simple as that! Remember, when I submitted to God and resisted throwing that verbal missile at my husband how the Enemy had no choice but to flee.

The Word is very clear about this, and we should apply this spiritual truth every time we start feeling tempted to accept and run with the Enemy's lies. The Devil is a stone-cold liar, and no truth resides in him; therefore, since we know the truth (Jesus), then we should not be falling for Satan's lies—ever!

> You are of your father the devil, and you want to do the desires of your father. He was a murderer from the beginning, and does not stand in the truth because there is no truth in him. Whenever he speaks a lie, he speaks from his own nature, for he is a liar and the father of lies. (John 8:44)

I declare that those who have walked in the fear of the Devil and the things of darkness come out of that place in the name of Jesus. I declare that you would have a Christ encounter that will cause you to step into your full identity as a son or daughter or God. May you be endued with courage and boldness to walk out your God-given purposes on the earth, and I declare that you will pull down the very resources of the open heaven before you, shut up the forces of evil around you, and boldly advance God's kingdom in the earth!

For those who know their identity in Christ and recognize that they are the Devil's master, I declare that you will enter into a new dimension of the things in the Spirit. I declare that you will vigorously seek Holy Spirit about releasing even greater dimensions of God's glory over every square inch of the sphere of your authority, which is the earth. May the Lord stretch your tent pegs even further and cause you to enter into new places where you will generously release His glory and bring transformation to those new places.

May you be saturated with the knowledge of God's love, and may He cause you to walk in new dimensions of grace and favor. I declare that you will experience even greater measures of knowledge, wisdom, and understanding so that you may know what the perfect will of God is for your life. May you also be able to discern the traps of the Enemy and resist his every attack. May you see and wisely counter his every move so that you will become the very person God created you to be and thus complete every assignment you've been given. In Jesus's mighty name! Amen.

Chapter

It's a New Day!

Do not remember the former things, nor consider the things of old. Behold, I will do a new thing, now it shall spring forth; Shall you not know it? I will even make a road in the wilderness and rivers in the desert. (Is. 43:18–19)

For the word of God is living and powerful, and sharper than any two-edged sword, piercing even to the division of soul and spirit, and of joints and marrow, and is a discerner of the thoughts and intents of the heart. (Heb. 4:12)

It's a New Day—What I Heard the Lord Say

At this point in the book, I hope you are deeply encouraged to quickly move forward into the new places that God has for His kingdom kids!

Early one morning, I knew that the Lord had a word He wanted me to release to the body of Christ. Sure, this word was given to me on a personal level too, but this was a corporate word, meant to encourage the greater body of Christ. The Lord said:

You are in a great time of a fervent and effectual "open door." In this season, things that were previously shut up are now being released and are now accessible in the spirit realm.

All you have to do is pull down those things that I am generously releasing to you. New resources are abundantly available to those who are willing to enter in. No longer will the blinders that have been so firmly in place blind My people from seeing those things plainly in front of them in this new place. No longer will My people be bound by the snares and traps of the Enemy. Those things they blindly stumbled into have caused them to draw further and further away from My Truth, My Son.

In this new season—the open-door season—I am showing My people how to come back in proper alignment with Me. In that place, there is an abundance of every provision needed for you to fulfill the purposes I've created you to fulfill. Your lives are so precious to Me—so precious that My Son's blood was spilled so that you can be reconciled to Me. That which once separated has now been removed, and you have been restored to your original design. You were created in Our image, which means you have creative ability, great authority, and the power to call those things that be not as though they were.

I equipped you with faith. Remember—a mustard seed of faith is all you need. It's the mightiest of all seeds and outgrows all the other seeds. It's the smallest in stature but mighty in its manifestation.

Don't ever be led into a thinking pattern that allows you to believe that you can't do anything, you are not anything, or you'll never be anything. You are in Me and I in you; therefore, you can do all things through Me—all things!

The season of doubting and negativity is over. You will be equipped with an abundance of hope and belief and an abundance of peace and joy, and it will be the norm—despite how dark some things may look. The days of discouragement are done. I Myself am your encourager, and since I reside in you and you abide in Me, there should be always sufficient hope and courage to do and go through anything and everything before you. Keep your eyes squarely fixed on Me and not the problem. When you see My greatness and glory, then the problem will look to you as it does to Me—teeny-weenie.

You'll be able to leap over things that were insurmountable in times past. You'll be shocked at how easy things can be when you rely on Me and the Christ in you—to cause you to sail through what's before you. Then and only then will you be able to count it all joy when various trials are before you. You'll look at them so differently. You'll see Me in the problem and not the problem itself, and definitely not the Enemy! He's such a poser and an impostor who wants all the credit and glory for what you're going through. If you keep your eyes on the problem, or worse, the Enemy, then you'll never be able to see what I am up to and how I desire to reposition you so that you can access all that I have for you—here at the King's table!

Come and eat. Eat to the fullest and then go out and share your food and feed My sheep. Feed My sheep; feed My sheep. If you are not eating from My table, come and eat. Don't lament and fret about the table you've been dining from. Simply leave—get up from there and come to Me. I'll take you by the hand and bring you to My table. No need to be fearful—let Me do it, because when I do a thing, then that thing is done and done. Come and eat. Be greedy about it. A starving man doesn't concern himself with who else is at the table or worry about manners or what people think. He eats like a ravenous pig because he's starving and hungry for real food—righteous, everlasting, and living food—the food that satisfies for a lifetime. You'll never hunger when you eat this way.

Be filled with all that I've already laid before you—and live. Be encouraged, My people. The season of lamenting and mourning is over. A new and prosperous season is here—right here and right now.

Those who enter in will be completely satisfied and lack no good thing. Come to the table and eat. Be merry. Be joyful and then spread that to all those in your sphere.

It's a new day, My people. The time is now!

—Papa God

My Declaration for You!

May this powerful word bless you mightily, just as it has blessed me and my family! I declare that you would receive this word with an open heart and an open mind, and may you take and eat of this word until it becomes part of you, flesh on the inside of you. I declare that you will be encouraged from the reading of this word, and may you have a deep desire to pursue your new or upgraded position at the King's table.

Lord, I declare that You will ignite a new passion and fire deep within our spiritual man. May that passion and fire blaze hot for You and the things of Your kingdom. Lord, we thank You for stirring such a great hunger and thirst within us that will cause us to operate in brand-new ways. May the things of the old no longer be considered because You are doing a new thing! We thank You that we can easily step into these new things and learn to walk in the new paths that You have created for us. Father, we thank You that as we walk in these new paths, we will be positioned such that others will be drawn to us, and as a result, they will know Your amazing love.

Holy Spirit, we thank You for being our Helper and for leading us into *all truth*. Show us how to connect with the Father and Christ Jesus when we engage in Your Prayer Pattern. We thank You that You have *already* given us ears to clearly hear and eyes to vividly see what You are doing in the heavenly places. May we *boldly* declare those things You speak to us into the earth, exactly as You have spoken. We declare that what You speak to us in the heavenly places will accomplish the purposes for which those words were sent, and may they never return to you void! Let *Your will* be done on earth as it is in heaven!

Lord, we thank You for changing us from the inside out, and I declare that we will see those changes daily. As we come into the fullness of all that You have for us, I declare that we would accomplish great and mighty things for Your name's sake. May we advance Your kingdom in the earth and release the very resources of heaven over *every situation* we face. I declare that every circumstance, problem, and anything not lined up with Your Word will bow its knee in the mighty Name of Jesus. Amen.

Chapter 15

It's Not Over—It's Only the Beginning

"All this," said David, "the Lord made me understand
in writing by His hand upon me, all the details of this
pattern." (1 Chron. 28:19 NASB)

Looking Back

Here we are at the end, but it's not really the end; it's only the beginning. The Prayer Pattern has completely changed our family's lives over the last two years. What started out as a daily prayer and declaration between my mom and me has now turned into daily calls with my 92-year-old grandmother, mom and dad, my two sisters, a great-granddaughter, other friends and family, and, me. The Prayer Pattern that God gave my mom and me was powerful when it was just the two of us praying, but since the others joined the call more than a year and a half ago, things have gone to a completely new level. The love, wisdom, compassion, and power coming out of my sister is nothing short of supernatural.

God so radically transformed our family relationships that I can hardly believe that there were any issues among us before. For nearly thirty years, relations were never great, but the two years prior to starting our prayer call, the relationship that my parents, other family members and I had with my sister and her family was virtually nonexistent. When we thought that things would never change, God had a totally different idea. When things were so bad that the fear of my sister's dying became a sad reality among a few family members, God was ready to do something big! When my mom and I were completely humbled by the gravity of it all, Holy Spirit came to the rescue with a plan that worked.

Once we came in line with God's will and began declaring what He led us to declare from the heavenly places—the throne room of God—*everything* changed. We came to realize that God was not going to magically change our situation, but He wanted *us* to co-labor with Him and Christ Jesus and declare *His will* over this situation. Christ gave us the authority and power to bring change to other situations, but we had neglected to apply this truth in this particular situation. The chief reasons for that were discouragement, unbelief, judgment, hardness of heart, passivity, apathy, and elements of hopelessness. Fortunately, Holy Spirit brought to light all of things that were firmly hidden—those things that ensnared us and kept us from stepping into the victory that was already ours but wasn't within our grasp.

After we started walking in our true identities in Christ Jesus and were led by Holy Spirit, we began seeing the outflow of His love, grace, and power over this situation. We then had the courage, faith, compassion, hope, and all the internal fortitude we needed to see this situation change—*once and for all.* No more weak and pitiful prayers. No more discouragement and hopelessness. No more passivity and apathy. No more judgment and hardness of heart. No more fear and anxiety that this situation would be this way until we die. The truth is that once we lined up with God's Word and His will, we entered into the most exciting period of our lives—and it only gets better from here!

The Prayer Pattern detailed in this book is but one small piece of living a victorious Christian life. As such, this is why I spent more time outlining many of the spiritual truths that take us into the victory that Christ secured over two thousand years ago. We can pray and declare until we are blue in the face, but chances are that we will not see the fullness of all that God has for us if we don't know or are not walking in the knowledge that we

- need to have a change of mind when we become discouraged or give up hope,
- need to pray and declare *from* the throne room of God and not throw up begging prayers,
- need to know who we are in Christ Jesus,
- have a Helper and are not alone,
- were made to dominate, right from creation,
- already have the victory,
- can truly hear God's voice,
- get to powerfully declare over our circumstances and watch them change,
- get to partner with God to see His will performed in the earth as He declares it to us in the heavenly places,
- are to keep our eyes fixed on God and *not* on our circumstances, and
- are to *never* shrink back or be afraid of the Devil because he is already defeated.

Looking Ahead

Now that you have the Prayer Pattern strategy and very important, necessary truths that will lead you straight to victory in every area of your life, it's time to put all of this in action. Allow God's grace to generously flow over you so that you can simply receive all of this without the struggles that you may have had in times past. I'm declaring that you will be highly motivated to have a deeper and more intimate relationship with our Father, Christ Jesus, and His Holy Spirit. As you put the Prayer Pattern to the test, I believe that you and your prayer partner(s) will be able to easily operate from the throne room to access all that God has waiting there for you. May the ears of your understanding be open so that you can hear everything that Holy Spirit speaks over your circumstances. I declare that your eyes will be so wide open that you will see everything from a fresh and new perspective, and you will be able to easily identify all the places where God is working on your behalf.

The Power of the Prophetic

Weeks before I began writing this book, God showed me a vision of where He wanted to take *Prayer Pattern*. He said that the *Prayer Pattern* would become a movement, and it would be global. He showed me something so huge that it almost scared me—almost. He told me to wisely steward all of this and be led by Holy Spirit in every step that I take. Additionally, I was told to start praying for the future readers of *Prayer Pattern*. I even had a vision of people in Africa reading this book, so I prayed for them as well. Every chapter was a product of Holy Spirit, and they contain some very important truths that He wants you to know for this season and this time for *Prayer Pattern*. This is not by any means an exhaustive look at prayer, nor is it really anything new.

The Lord's Prayer is the true prayer pattern. Matthew 6:9–10 says, "In this manner, therefore, pray: Our Father in heaven, hallowed be Your name. Your kingdom come. Your will be done on earth as it is in heaven." He told us that we have a Father and that He resides in heaven. He said that His name is made holy. Jesus declared that His kingdom come and His will be done. Where was this supposed to take place? Jesus said it was to take place on this earth where we reside. How was this supposed to happen? Exactly *as it is* in heaven! So how it is in heaven, we are to declare that it be done in the earth. It is with our mouths and our actions *through Holy Spirit* that this is accomplished. This, my friends, is the true prayer pattern, and it was given to us more than two thousand years ago.

This is not difficult or complicated; we need only *to believe* that this is how God's kingdom operates and to co-labor with Him in the heavenly places. Remember—we physically live here in the earth, but our spiritual citizenship is in the heavenly places—right at the throne of God. We therefore operate in two dimensions at the same time, and this should be a normal practice of every single believer. We are God's ambassadors here on earth, and we get to establish His kingdom in the earth. It starts with us individually. Then it moves into our families, our churches (the body of Christ), our cities, our regions, our nations, and then into other nations. We cannot establish the government of God anywhere else if His government, His kingdom, is not first established on the inside of us. Just a reminder: we cannot give away *anything* that we first don't possess ourselves.

Before I close, I wanted to share a prophetic word that I received from our pastor's wife, who also happens to operate in a strong gift of prophecy. This prophetic word was given to me exactly ten days before all of the mess with my sister occurred. When she released this word, I thought it was related to business, and I was all ready to jump on it for that purpose. Little did I know that this word was for the Prayer Pattern and was a guide of sorts; it helped me to have a laser focus by documenting this whole process and helped me bring it to completion.

In fact, when Holy Spirit had just given us the Prayer Pattern strategy, my mom suggested that I start documenting everything that transpired from there. She said that she could not believe that she would suggest something like that, but she just knew that God was going to do something mighty in this situation and we therefore should be documenting everything. I'm not sure about this, but I would think that when people go through some kind of terrible situation and then experience a subsequent victory, it's at *that* point that they think about documenting what happened, not when they are still in the beginning of the mess and there are no visible signs to indicate change of any kind. It wasn't until a few weeks later that I listened to that prophetic word again and realized that it was for this particular situation and for bringing the Prayer Pattern to life, *not* for application in the business arena. I'm not saying that it couldn't be used for that later, but after reading it, you tell me what you think. This is what she said.

> The Lord says, "Tracy, go for it, go for it, go for it. Don't stop, don't stop, go for it, go for it. There is no limitation here; go for it. What I have put in you to be, what I have put in you mostly to do, what I have given you, the patterns and designs that I've given you in your head, bring them about. Declare even; put them on paper so that you may run with them so that others may see it.

Bring those designs out of your head. You have even designs for what people ought to be; you have designs, designs for what people ought to do. You have designs—creative designs of things that have not yet existed in those ways before. Put it out and declare "life" to them. Even as you put something on paper, declare "life, life, life," to that and see it rise up.

I'm seeing even as someone makes an architectural drawing and then all of a sudden they make that model, and it becomes something more, that model will become a place to build on and for others to embrace and to bring it to reality.

I've put patterns and designs in you, daughter. I put designs in you, and as you write them down and declare life to them, they *will* come forth. This is a new day and you say, Well, Lord, I've been doing some of that already.... Why is it a new day?

I say it's a new day because I opened extraordinary resources to you, extraordinary resources, connections, connections for finance, connections for skill, connections for building material, connections for experience and education and opportunities that other people have that you need—what they have, the know-how that they have. I will bring you those resources and put them in your hands. So *make* it come forth, make it come forth. You have the ability to make it come forth!

When God gives us a prophetic word, we have the opportunity to believe His Word and then act on it. Many of you have had prophetic words spoken over your lives and have yet to see them come to pass. However, today is a new day, and I encourage you to get out those prophetic words and read them again with the new eyes that God has given you. Take that prophetic word into the throne room and declare it back to Him. Ask Holy Spirit to give you insight into your prophetic words and to show you how to enter into the promises contained in that word.

If you have never had a prophetic word, simply ask Holy Spirit to give you one. All you have to do is sit down with a journal or a piece of paper and listen for what He has to say. It may be challenging in the beginning, but I promise you, He can't wait to speak to you and tell you of the wonderful things He has planned for you. Remember to listen for the thoughts that are not your thoughts. You will be able to think your own thoughts, but you will also very clearly hear Him speaking. When you do, *write it down*! You will be amazed and overjoyed when you read what He has to say.

By reading this book, you are a witness to the manifestation and fulfillment of my prophetic word. Keep in mind that this prophetic word was declared from the throne room of God, and *He* is the one who brought it to pass. I have never written a book before, and quite frankly, I barely graduated from high school. When I went to college, I did not know how to write a paper. You think that's bad? Within the last year, I was threatened in a job that if I did not get my "writing act" together, I would not be able to keep my employment there. Embarrassing as these things were at the time, it only goes to show that God Himself qualifies the called. Ha! The good news is that through God's Holy Spirit and through Christ who lives on the inside of us, we can do all of the things that He calls us to do. I say this to encourage you that no matter what you have or don't have, it's God who will help you get to where you need to be.

Be Encouraged

May you experience radical God encounters; increased knowledge, wisdom, and understanding of who you are in Christ Jesus; and help in all situations from Holy Spirit. May you also walk in the power and authority that you've been given to enforce the victory that Christ secured over two thousand years ago.

May you boldly go forth from this day on and accomplish everything that God calls you to do. I declare that you would experience transformation within yourself as well as your circumstances; and with that newfound freedom, I declare that you would rise up and begin praying and declaring over others in your sphere of influence. May the Lord work numerous miracles, signs, and wonders through your hands, and may He ignite a fire in you that would cause an explosion of his glory to radiate through you and into the earth. May God's will be done in your life and in this earth just as He declares it to you in the heavenly places! Amen.

I leave you with this powerful Scripture, known as the Prayer for Spiritual Wisdom.

> Therefore I also, after I heard of your faith in the Lord Jesus and your love for all the saints, *do not cease to give thanks for you, making mention of you in my prayers*: that the God of our Lord Jesus Christ, the Father of glory, may give to you the spirit of wisdom and revelation in the knowledge of Him, the eyes of your understanding being enlightened; *that you may know what is the hope of His calling*, what are the riches of the glory of His inheritance in the saints, and what is the exceeding greatness of His power toward us who believe, according to the working of His mighty power which He worked in Christ when He raised Him from the dead and seated Him at His right hand in the heavenly places, *far above all principality and power and might and dominion*, and every name that is named, *not only in this age but also in that which is to come*. (Eph. 1:15–21, emphasis added)

Amen.

Chapter 16

Prayer Pattern
Foundational Scriptures

"All this," said David, "the Lord made me understand in writing, by His hand upon me, all the works of these plans." (1 Chron. 28:19)

The Process of Resignation

So we see that they could not enter in because of unbelief. (Prov. 13:12)

Hope deferred makes the heart sick, but when the desire comes, it is a tree of life. (Heb. 3:19)

A Change of Mind

Now I rejoice, not that you were made sorry, but that your sorrow led to repentance. For you were made sorry in a godly manner, that you might suffer loss from us in nothing. For godly sorrow produces repentance leading to salvation, not to be regretted; but the sorrow of the world produces death. For observe this very thing—that you sorrowed in a godly manner: What diligence it produced in you, what clearing of yourselves, what indignation, what fear, what vehement desire, what zeal, what vindication! In all things you proved yourselves to be clear in this matter. (2 Cor. 7:9–11)

But one testified in a certain place, saying: "What is man that You are mindful of him, or the son of man that You take care of him? You have made him a little lower than the angels; You have crowned him with glory and honor, and set him over the works of Your hands. (Heb. 2:6–8)

"If? There are no 'ifs' among believers. Anything can happen." No sooner were the words out of his mouth than the father cried, "Then I believe. Help me with my doubts!" (Mark 9:23 MSG)

Peter fairly exploded with his good news: "It's God's own truth, nothing could be plainer: God plays no favorites! It makes no difference who you are or where you're from—if you want God and are ready to do as he says, the door is open. The Message he sent to the children of Israel—that through Jesus Christ everything is being put together again—well, he's doing it everywhere, among everyone. (Mark 10:34–36 MSG)

What Exactly Is the Prayer Pattern?

In this manner, therefore, pray: Our Father in heaven, Hallowed be Your name. Your kingdom come. Your will be done on earth as it is in heaven. (Matt. 6:9–10)

Let us therefore come boldly to the throne of grace that we may obtain mercy and find grace to help in time of need. (Heb. 4:16)

Then you will call upon Me and go and pray to Me, and I will listen to you. And you will seek Me and find Me, when you search for Me with all your heart. (Jer. 29:12–13)

Be anxious for nothing, but in everything by prayer and supplication, with thanksgiving, let your requests be made known to God; and the peace of God, which surpasses all understanding, will guard your hearts and minds through Christ Jesus. (Phil. 4:6–7)

Even when we were dead in trespasses, (He) made us alive together with Christ (by grace you have been saved), and raised us up together, and made us sit together in the heavenly places in Christ Jesus. (Eph. 2:5–6)

In Him also we have obtained an inheritance, being predestined according to the purpose of Him who works all things according to the counsel of His will. (Eph. 1:11)

Blessed be the God and Father of our Lord Jesus Christ, who has blessed us with every spiritual blessing in the heavenly places in Christ. (Eph. 1:3)

Therefore He is able also to save forever those who draw near to God through Him, since He always lives to make intercession for them. (Heb. 7:25)

I pray that the eyes of your heart may be enlightened, so that you will know what is the hope of His calling, what are the riches of the glory of His inheritance in the saints, and what is the surpassing greatness of His power toward us who believe. Which He worked in Christ when He raised Him from the dead and seated Him at His right hand in the heavenly places, far above all principality and power and might and dominion, and every name that is named, not only in this age but also in that which is to come. And He put all things under His feet, and gave Him to be head over all things to the church, which is His body, the fullness of Him who fills all in all. (Eph. 1:18–23)

Prayer Pattern Disclaimer

Ask, and it will be given to you; seek, and you will find; knock, and it will be opened to you. For everyone who asks receives, and he who seeks finds, and to him who knocks it will be opened. Or what man is there among you who, if his son asks for bread, will give him a stone? Or if he asks for a fish, will he give him a serpent? If you then, being evil, know how to give good gifts to your children, how much more will your Father who is in heaven give good things to those who ask Him! (Matt. 7:7–11)

And whatever we ask we receive from Him, because we keep His commandments and do those things that are pleasing in His sight. (1 John 3:22)

But the fruit of the Spirit is love, joy, peace, longsuffering, kindness, goodness, faithfulness, gentleness, self-control. Against such there is no law. And those who are Christ's have crucified the flesh with its passions and desires. If we live in the Spirit, let us also walk in the Spirit. (Gal. 5:22–25)

But seek first the kingdom of God and His righteousness, and all these things shall be added to you. (Matt. 6:33)

For by grace you have been saved through faith, and that not of yourselves; it is the gift of God, not of works, lest anyone should boast. (Eph. 2:8–9)

For the Lord God is a sun and shield; The Lord will give grace and glory; No good thing will He withhold from those who walk uprightly. (Ps. 84:11)

And He said to me, "My grace is sufficient for you, for My strength is made perfect in weakness." Therefore most gladly I will rather boast in my infirmities, that the power of Christ may rest upon me. (2 Cor. 12:9)

The Heavenly Places and the White House

Even when we were dead in trespasses, made us alive together with Christ (by grace you have been saved), and raised us up together, and made us sit together in the heavenly places in Christ Jesus, that in the ages to come He might show the exceeding riches of His grace in His kindness toward us in Christ Jesus. (Eph. 2:5–7)

I pray that the eyes of your heart may be enlightened, so that you will know what is the hope of His calling, what are the riches of the glory of His inheritance in the saints, and what is the surpassing greatness of His power toward us who believe. And what is the exceeding greatness of His power toward us who believe, according to the working of His mighty power which He worked in Christ when He raised Him from the dead and seated Him at His right hand in the heavenly places, far above all principality and power and might and dominion, and every name that is named, not only in this age but also in that which is to come. (Eph. 1:18–21)

Put on the whole armor of God, that you may be able to stand against the wiles of the devil. (Eph. 6:11)

Blessed be the God and Father of our Lord Jesus Christ, who has blessed us with every spiritual blessing in the heavenly places in Christ ... having predestined us to adoption as sons by Jesus Christ to Himself, according to the good pleasure of His will, to the praise of the glory of His grace, by which He made us accepted in the Beloved. ... In Him also we have obtained an inheritance, being predestined according to the purpose of Him who works all things according to the counsel of His will. (Eph. 1:3, 5–6, 11)

For He shall give His angels charge over you, to keep you in all your ways. (Ps. 91:11)

First Things First: You Were Made to Dominate!

Then God said, "Let Us make man in Our image, according to Our likeness; let them have dominion over the fish of the sea, over the birds of the air, and over the cattle, over all the earth and over every creeping thing that creeps on the earth." So God created man in His own image; in the image of God He created him; male and female He created them. Then God blessed them, and God said to them, "Be fruitful and multiply; fill the earth and subdue it; have dominion over the fish of the sea, over the birds of the air, and over every living thing that moves on the earth." (Gen. 1:26–28)

What is man that You are mindful of him, and the son of man that You visit him? ... You have made him to have dominion over the works of Your hands; You have put all things under his feet. (Ps. 8:4, 6)

For we are His workmanship, created in Christ Jesus for good works, which God prepared beforehand that we should walk in them. (Eph. 2:10)

I pray that the eyes of your heart may be enlightened, so that you will know what is the hope of His calling, what are the riches of the glory of His inheritance in the saints, and what is the surpassing greatness of His power toward us who believe. These are in accordance with the working of the strength of His might which He worked in Christ when He raised Him from the dead and seated Him at His right hand in the heavenly places, far above all principality and power and might and dominion, and every name that is named, not only in this age but also in that which is to come. And He put all things under His feet, and gave Him to be head over all things to the church, which is His body, the fullness of Him who fills all in all. (Eph. 1:18–23)

Because of that sacrifice, we know that through death He might destroy him who had the power of death, that is, the devil. (Heb. 2:14 NASB)

But thanks be to God, who gives us the victory through our Lord Jesus Christ. (1 Cor. 15:57)

Yet in all these things we are more than conquerors through Him who loved us (Rom. 8:37)

My brethren, count it all joy when you fall into various trials, knowing that the testing of your faith produces patience. But let patience have its perfect work, that you may be perfect and complete, lacking nothing. (James 1:2–4)

For there is no partiality with God. (Rom. 2:11)

Victory Is Yours!

For the Lord your God is the one who goes with you to fight for you against your enemies to give you the victory. (Duet. 20:4 NIV)

Now thanks be to God who always leads us in triumph in Christ, and through us diffuses the fragrance of His knowledge in every place. (2 Cor. 2:14)

Yet in all these things we are more than conquerors through Him who loved us. (Rom. 8:37)

And we know that all things work together for good to those who love God, to those who are the called according to His purpose. (Rom. 8:28)

And from the days of John the Baptist until now the kingdom of heaven suffers violence, and the violent take it by force. (Matt. 11:12)

But He was wounded for our transgressions, He was bruised for our iniquities; the chastisement for our peace was upon Him, and by His stripes we are healed. (Is. 53:5)

And take the helmet of salvation, and the sword of the Spirit, which is the word of God. (Eph. 6:17)

I have told you these things, so that in me you may have peace. In this world you will have trouble. But take heart! I have overcome the world. (Matt. 16:33)

You are of God, little children, and have overcome them, because He who is in you is greater than he who is in the world. (1 John 4:4)

My brethren, count it all joy when you fall into various trials, knowing that the testing of your faith produces patience. But let patience have its perfect work, that you may be perfect and complete, lacking nothing. (James 1:2–4)

You Are Not Alone—You Have a Helper!

And I will pray the Father, and He will give you another Helper, that He may abide with you forever—the Spirit of truth, whom the world cannot receive, because it neither sees Him nor knows Him; but you know Him, for He dwells with you and will be in you. (John 14:16–17)

However, when He, the Spirit of truth, has come, He will guide you into all truth; for He will not speak on His own authority, but whatever He hears He will speak; and He will tell you things to come. He will glorify Me, for He will take of what is Mine and declare it to you. All things that the Father has are Mine. Therefore I said that He will take of Mine and declare it to you. (John 16:13–15)

Nevertheless when one turns to the Lord, the veil is taken away. Now the Lord is the Spirit; and where the Spirit of the Lord is, there is liberty. (2 Cor. 3:16–17)

But as it is written: "Eye has not seen, nor ear heard, nor have entered into the heart of man the things which God has prepared for those who love Him." But God has revealed them to us through His Spirit. For the Spirit searches all things, yes, the deep things of God. For what man knows the things of a man except the spirit of the man which is in him? Even so no one knows the things of God except the Spirit of God. Now we have received, not the spirit of the world, but the Spirit who is from God, that we might know the things that have been freely given to us by God. (1 Cor. 2:9–12)

Let the heavens declare His righteousness for God Himself is Judge. (Ps. 50:6)

For the Lord is our Judge, the Lord is our Lawgiver, the Lord is our King; He will save us. (Is. 33:22)

Finally, there is laid up for me the crown of righteousness, which the Lord, the righteous Judge, will give to me on that day, and not to me only but also to all who have loved His appearing. (2 Tim. 4:8)

But God has revealed them to us through His Spirit. For the Spirit searches all things, yes, the deep things of God. (1 Cor. 2:10)

But the Helper, the Holy Spirit, whom the Father will send in My name, He will teach you all things, and bring to your remembrance all things that I (Jesus) said to you. (John 14:26)

Likewise the Spirit also helps in our weaknesses. For we do not know what we should pray for as we ought, but the Spirit Himself makes intercession for us with groanings which cannot be uttered. Now He who searches the hearts knows what the mind of the Spirit is, because He makes intercession for the saints according to the will of God. (Rom. 8:26–27)

The Spirit of truth, whom the world cannot receive, because it neither sees Him nor knows Him; but you know Him, for He dwells with you and will be in you. (John 14:17)

Jesus answered and said to him, "If anyone loves Me, he will keep My word; and My Father will love him, and We will come to him and make Our home with him. (John 14:23)

The Spirit of the Lord God is upon Me, because the Lord has anointed Me to preach good tidings to the poor; He has sent Me to heal the brokenhearted, to proclaim liberty to the captives, and the opening of the prison to those who are bound. (Is. 61:1)

For all who are being led by the Spirit of God, these are sons of God. For you have not received a spirit of slavery leading to fear again, but you have received a spirit of adoption as sons by which we cry out, "Abba! Father!" (Rom. 8:14–15 NASB)

But Jesus looked at them and said to them, "With men this is impossible, but with God all things are possible." (Matt. 19:26)

Learning to Hear God's Voice

My sheep hear My voice, and I know them, and they follow Me. (John 10:27)

O earth, earth, earth, hear the word of the Lord! (Jer. 22:29 NKJV)

Behold, the former things have come to pass, and new things I declare; before they spring forth I tell you of them. (Is. 42:9)

I am the good shepherd. ... (John 10:11) But he who enters by the door is the shepherd of the sheep. To him the doorkeeper opens, and the sheep hear his voice; and he calls his own sheep by name and leads them out. And when he brings out his own sheep, he goes before them; and the sheep follow him, for they know his voice. (John 10:2–4)

Trust in the Lord with all your heart, and lean not on your own understanding; in all your ways acknowledge Him, and He shall direct your paths. (Prov. 3:5–6)

But He said, "More than that, blessed are those who hear the word of God and keep it!" (Luke 11:28)

However, when He, the Spirit of truth, has come, He will guide you into all truth; for He will not speak on His own authority, but whatever He hears He will speak; and He will tell you things to come. (John 16:13)

For God does not show favoritism. (Rom. 2:11 NIV)

Open Your Mouth and Declare!

You will also declare a thing, and it will be established for you; so light will shine on your ways. (Job 22:28)

I will tell you, hear me; what I have seen I will declare ... (Job 15:17)

Death and life are in the power of the tongue, and those who love it will eat its fruit. (Prov. 18:21)

God said, "Let there be light" and there was light. (Gen. 1:3)

By the word of the Lord the heavens were made, and all the host of them by the breath of His mouth.... For He spoke and it was done; He commanded, and it stood fast. (Ps. 33:6, 9)

So shall My word be that goes forth from My mouth; it shall not return to Me void, but it shall accomplish what I please, and it shall prosper in the thing for which I sent it. (Is. 55:11)

Please receive instruction from His mouth and establish His words in your heart. (Job 22:28 NASB)

Then Jesus said, "God's kingdom is like seed thrown on a field by a man who then goes to bed and forgets about it. The seed sprouts and grows—he has no idea how it happens. The earth does it all without his help: first a green stem of grass, then a bud, then the ripened grain. When the grain is fully formed, he reaps—harvest time! (Mark 4:26–29 MSG)

Out of the ground the Lord God formed every beast of the field and every bird of the air, and brought them to Adam to see what he would call them. And whatever Adam called each living creature, that was its name. (Gen. 2:19)

Therefore, if anyone is in Christ, he is a new creation; old things have passed away; behold, all things have become new. Now all things are of God, who has reconciled us to Himself through Jesus Christ, and has given us the ministry of reconciliation. (2 Cor. 5:17–18)

Now the serpent was more cunning than any beast of the field which the Lord God had made. And he said to the woman, "Has God indeed said, 'You shall not eat of every tree of the garden'?" (Gen. 3:1)

On Earth as It Is in Heaven

Your kingdom come. Your will be done on earth as it is in heaven. (Matt. 6:10)

The Lord has established His throne in heaven, and His kingdom rules over all. (Ps. 103:19)

Blessed be the God and Father of our Lord Jesus Christ, who has blessed us with every spiritual blessing in the heavenly places in Christ. (Eph. 1:3)

I will give you the keys of the kingdom of heaven; and whatever you bind (declare to be improper and unlawful) on earth must be what is already bound in heaven; and whatever you loose (declare lawful) on earth must be what is already loosed in heaven. (Matt. 16:19 AMP)

And when you pray, do not use vain repetitions as the heathen do. For they think that they will be heard for their many words. Therefore do not be like them. For your Father knows the things you have need of before you ask Him. (Matt. 6:7–8)

If a son asks for bread from any father among you, will he give him a stone? Or if he asks for a fish, will he give him a serpent instead of a fish? Or if he asks for an egg, will he offer him a scorpion? If you then, being evil, know how to give good gifts to your children, how much more will your heavenly Father give the Holy Spirit to those who ask Him! (Luke 11:11–13)

So I say to you, ask, and it will be given to you; seek, and you will find; knock, and it will be opened to you. (Luke 11:9)

But the natural man does not receive the things of the Spirit of God, for they are foolishness to him; nor can he know them, because they are spiritually discerned. (1 Cor. 2:14)

And because you are sons, God has sent forth the Spirit of His Son into your hearts, crying out, "Abba, Father!" Therefore you are no longer a slave but a son, and if a son, then an heir of God through Christ. (Gal. 4:6–7)

No longer do I call you servants, for a servant does not know what his master is doing; but I have called you friends, *for all things that I heard from My Father I have made known to you.* (John 15:15, emphasis added)

So then, after the Lord had spoken to them, He was received up into heaven, and sat down at the right hand of God. (Mark 16:19)

Twelve Kingdom Truths

1. For the kingdom of God is not eating and drinking, but righteousness and peace and joy in the Holy Spirit. (Rom. 14:17)
2. For the kingdom of God is not in word but in power. (1 Cor. 4:20)
3. But He said to them, "I must preach the kingdom of God to the other cities also, because for this purpose I have been sent." (Luke 4:43)
4. ... and saying, "The time is fulfilled, and the kingdom of God is at hand. Repent, and believe in the gospel." (Mark 1:15)
5. Jesus answered and said to him, "Most assuredly, I say to you, unless one is born again, he cannot see the kingdom of God." (John 3:3)
6. Jesus answered, "Most assuredly, I say to you, unless one is born of water and the Spirit, he cannot enter the kingdom of God." (John 3:5)
7. Assuredly, I say to you, whoever does not receive the kingdom of God as a little child will by no means enter it. (Mark 10:15)
8. But seek first the kingdom of God and His righteousness, and all these things shall be added to you. (Matt. 6:33)
9. And I bestow upon you a kingdom, just as My Father bestowed one upon Me. (Luke 22:29)
10. And He said, "To you it has been given to know the mysteries of the kingdom of God, but to the rest it is given in parables, that 'Seeing they may not see, And hearing they may not understand.'" (Luke 8:10)
11. And I will give you the keys of the kingdom of heaven, and whatever you bind on earth will be bound in heaven, and whatever you loose on earth will be loosed in heaven." (Matt. 16:19)
12. And as you go, preach, saying, "The kingdom of heaven is at hand." (Matt. 10:7)

Nor will they say, "See here!" or "See there!" For indeed, the kingdom of God is within you. (Luke 17:21)

Keep Your Eyes on God, Not the Circumstances

For momentary, light affliction is producing for us an eternal weight of glory far beyond all comparison, while we look not at the things which are seen, but at the things which are not seen; for the things which are seen are temporal, but the things which are not seen are eternal. (2 Cor. 4:17–18)

If then you were raised with Christ, seek those things which are above, where Christ is, sitting at the right hand of God. Set your mind on things above, not on things on the earth. (Col. 3:1–2)

My brethren, count it all joy when you fall into various trials, knowing that the testing of your faith produces patience. (James 1:2–3)

Don't Buy the Lie—The Devil Ain't All That!

Having disarmed principalities and powers, He made a public spectacle of them, triumphing over them in it. (Col. 2:15)

Inasmuch then as the children have partaken of flesh and blood, He Himself likewise shared in the same, that through death He might destroy him who had the power of death, that is, the devil, and release those who through fear of death were all their lifetime subject to bondage. (Heb. 2:14–15)

Above all, taking the shield of faith with which you will be able to quench all the fiery darts of the wicked one. (Eph. 6:16)

"Have I not commanded you? Be strong and of good courage; do not be afraid, nor be dismayed, for the Lord your God is with you wherever you go." (Joshua 1:9)

Rule in the midst of your enemies. (Ps. 110:2 NIV)

He has delivered us from the power of darkness and conveyed us into the kingdom of the Son of His love. (Col. 1:13)

But the Lord is faithful, who will establish you and guard you **from the evil one**. (2 Thess. 3:3)

Be sober, be vigilant; because your adversary the devil walks about like a roaring lion, seeking whom he may devour. (1 Peter 5:8)

How you are fallen from heaven, O Lucifer, son of the morning! How you are cut down to the ground, You who weakened the nations! For you have said in your heart: "I will ascend into heaven, I will exalt my throne above the stars of God; I will also sit on the mount of the congregation on the farthest sides of the north."... Yet you shall be brought down to Sheol, to the lowest depths of the Pit. Those who see you will gaze at you, And consider you, saying: "*Is* this the man who made the earth tremble, who shook kingdoms, who made the world as a wilderness and destroyed its cities, who did not open the house of his prisoners?" (Is. 14:12–13, 15–17)

So the great dragon was cast out, that serpent of old, called the Devil and Satan, who deceives the whole world; he was cast to the earth, and his angels were cast out with him. (Rev. 12:9)

And do not give the devil an opportunity. (Eph. 4:27 NASB)

Therefore submit to God. Resist the devil and he will flee from you. (James 4:7)

Above all, taking the shield of faith with which you will be able to quench all the fiery darts of the wicked one. (Eph. 6:16)

"No weapon that is formed against you will prosper; and every tongue that accuses you in judgment you will condemn. This is the heritage of the servants of the Lord, and their vindication is from Me," declares the Lord. (Is. 54:17 NASB)

You are of your father the devil, and you want to do the desires of your father. He was a murderer from the beginning, and does not stand in the truth because there is no truth in him. Whenever he speaks a lie, he speaks from his own nature, for he is a liar and the father of lies. (John 8:44 NASB)

It's a New Day!

Do not remember the former things, nor consider the things of old. Behold, I will do a new thing, now it shall spring forth; Shall you not know it? I will even make a road in the wilderness and rivers in the desert. (Is. 43:18–19)

For the word of God is living and powerful, and sharper than any two-edged sword, piercing even to the division of soul and spirit, and of joints and marrow, and is a discerner of the thoughts and intents of the heart. (Heb. 4:12)

It's Not Over—It's Only the Beginning

"All this," said David, "the Lord made me understand in writing by His hand upon me, all the details of this pattern." (1 Chron. 28:19 NASB)

Prayer for Spiritual Wisdom

Therefore I also, after I heard of your faith in the Lord Jesus and your love for all the saints, do not cease to give thanks for you, making mention of you in my prayers: that the God of our Lord Jesus Christ, the Father of glory, may give to you the spirit of wisdom and revelation in the knowledge of Him, the eyes of your understanding being enlightened; that you may know what is the hope of His calling, what are the riches of the glory of His inheritance in the saints, and what is the exceeding greatness of His power toward us who believe, according to the working of His mighty power which He worked in Christ when He raised Him from the dead and seated Him at His right hand in the heavenly places, far above all principality and power and might and dominion, and every name that is named, not only in this age but also in that which is to come. (Eph. 1:15–21)

Connect with the Prayer Pattern Movement

Join the movement and connect with us through any of the following channels:

Prayer Pattern.com Learn more about the Prayer Pattern movement, success stories, where we're headed in the future, newsletters, and creative wearables that show your connection to this kingdom movement.

Prayer Pattern Facebook Page Best place for real-time testimonials and questions. Tell us how God used this Prayer Pattern to change your life.

Prayer Pattern Twitter Account Powerful prayer declarations and updates- in 140 words or less!

Email: info@PrayerPattern.com
Visit our website, www.PrayerPattern.com.

71693443R10107

Made in the USA
Lexington, KY
22 November 2017